The Singing Bowl

MARY BURRITT CHRISTIANSEN POETRY SERIES

V. B. PRICE, SERIES EDITOR

Mary Burritt Christiansen Poetry Series

Also available in the University of New Mexico Press
Mary Burritt Christiansen Poetry Series:

Poets of the Non-Existent City: Los Angeles in the McCarthy Era
edited by Estelle Gershgoren Novak

Selected Poems of Gabriela Mistral edited by Ursula K. Le Guin

Deeply Dug In by R. L. Barth

Amulet Songs: Poems Selected and New by Lucile Adler

In Company: An Anthology of New Mexico Poets After 1960 edited
by Lee Bartlett, V. B. Price, and Dianne Edenfield Edwards

Tiempos Lejanos: Poetic Images from the Past by Nasario García

Refuge of Whirling Light by Mary Beath

*The River Is Wide/El río es ancho: Twenty Mexican Poets, a
Bilingual Anthology* edited and translated by Marlon L. Fick

A Scar Upon Our Voice by Robin Coffee

CrashBoomLove: A Novel in Verse by Juan Felipe Herrera

In a Dybbuk's Raincoat: Collected Poems by Bert Meyers

Rebirth of Wonder: Poems of the Common Life by
David M. Johnson

Broken and Reset: Selected Poems, 1966 to 2006 by V. B. Price

The Curvature of the Earth by Gene Frumkin and Alvaro Cardona-Hine

Derivative of the Moving Image by Jennifer Bartlett

Map of the Lost by Miriam Sagan

¿de Veras?: Young Voices from the National Hispanic Cultural Center edited by Mikaela Jae Renz and Shelle VanEtten-Luaces

A Bigger Boat: The Unlikely Success of the Albuquerque Poetry Slam Scene edited by Susan McAllister, Don McIver, Mikaela Renz, and Daniel S. Solis

A Poetry of Remembrance: New and Rejected Works by Levi Romero

The Welcome Table by Jay Udall

How Shadows Are Bundled by Anne Valley-Fox

Bolitas de oro: Poems of My Marble-Playing Days by Nasario García

Blood Desert: Witnesses, 1820–1880 by Renny Golden

Mary Burritt
Christiansen
Poetry Series

The Singing Bowl

❧

Joan Logghe

UNIVERSITY OF NEW MEXICO PRESS
ALBUQUERQUE

Dedicated to my grandchildren: reverberations
Galen Brook Haynes, Kaylee Sophia Logghe, and
Marcos Manuel Romero

© 2011 by University of New Mexico Press
All rights reserved. Published 2011
Printed in the United States of America
16 15 14 13 12 11   2 3 4 5 6 7

Library of Congress Cataloging-in-Publication Data
Logghe, Joan, 1947–
The singing bowl / Joan Logghe.
p. cm. — (Mary Burritt Christiansen poetry series)
ISBN 978-0-8263-4986-6 (paper : alk. paper)
I. Title.

PS3562.04498S56 2011
811'.54—dc22
                                        2010023088

> ... *I hear*
> *the song that carries my neighbor*
> *from one thing to the next:*
> Earth feeds us
> out of her empty bowl
> —Peter Levitt

Contents

Foreword

THE SINGING BOWL SHOWS US WHY so many readers over the years have fallen in love at first sight with Joan Logghe's poems. Her attentiveness to detail, her appreciative warmth, off-the-wall humor wrapped in kindness, her affection for the world, and her passionate and inclusive social conscience make her work irresistibly welcoming. She's been called a New Mexico treasure but, though she writes from the roots of the land she holds so closely, she's a writer whose humanity transcends location.

In one of the poems in *The Singing Bowl*, "On the Road in Green," she takes the reader across psychological and physical landscapes:

> All of the sudden hearts are green and green
> hearted we Dylan Thomas onto the shoulder of the road
> where we pull over and put our ear down to the soul
> listen to Anne Sexton and Sylvia, a gas lassitude,
> and pull ourselves up by our spiritual bootstraps and away
> from the drunks, the suicides, thinking my heart is the green
> model, circa Anytime, and motor off in Neal Cassady's last
> convertible, skipping Mexico and going straight
> to California. . . .

Through language Logghe is so intimately connected with the world at large that she's mastered the complex instrument of daily life, playing its melodies and fugues so they braid into its endless moments, everything from world-shaking politics to breakfast, shooting stars, convertibles, suicides, reverie, escape, and holding hands. When Logghe gives readings, her audiences are often boisterously happy and delighted with the renditions she gives of favorite poems. And other writers, like Natalie Goldberg, author of *Writing Down the Bones*, are so taken with her work they are unrestrained in their praise: "Joan Logghe is one of the most exciting poets in America today. Her words sing, slide, slip & jive. I love everything by Joan." Logghe's public persona is based on her poems, but is also enriched by her public service in prisons, with AIDS prevention in schools, and her work as a creative writing teacher and workshop leader.

The Singing Bowl's poems are hot-wired to the *metaphoric* open source of an imagination so attuned to the doings of time and what fills it that everything, even the most seemingly disparate events and objects, belong together in sound and meaning as they do in the flow of experience. There is no value hierarchy in the objects of the world:

> We drink from a well we dug inside our bodies.
> Egyptians call relationship *Invisible Painting*.
> He and I are incognito Rembrandts. We eat Van Gogh
> dinners sipping our Matisse wine. A loquacious chicken.
> . . . We plant a catalpa next to a yucca
> next to the vinca beside the ginkgo. On Paradise
> we feast. There are no enemies in the wild, each tree
> is perfect. The one called enemy becomes my teacher.

The craftsmanship of the poems fascinates other poets. She creates coherence among plurality without transitions, without obvious joinery, much as if the events of one second everywhere in the world were laid out before us and we could see and grasp the full profusion in its patterns and purposes. The world is woven of non sequiturs and the kinds of jokes that only the gods understand: "I named my last child Hope. I never had a last child," she writes in a poem called "True or False." "Television is the Golden Calf I read about / in Sabbath School. My teacher lied. // We live on the northern edge of the

Sonorous desert. / Armageddon is a small lizard that reconstitutes at first rain. / Turtles have an aversion to helium because they are heavyhearted."

Logghe's poetic gifts allow her to create poems that have the authenticity of collages of found objects. Images and metaphors are laid side by side to create a possibility of meaning that they make room for. Logghe's poems are so personal to so many readers, I think, because she is respectful of their imaginations, leaving room for them to use her poems to explore emotional meaning in their lives. Apart from their catalytic accessibility, Logghe's poems are so beautifully made, so rich in possibility and devotion to the exceptions and patterns of the world that they give the reader the means to approach the energy and order hidden in the eye of the cosmos, everywhere you look.

—V. B. Price, Albuquerque

Acknowledgments

Some of these poems have appeared in the following publications, both in print and online:

"Blanco Ascending" in *Poets of the American West*, Many Voices Press

"After Horses, Horses," "The Singing Bowl," and "War and Morning" in online chapbooks of *Santa Fe Poetry Broadside*

"The Seven Wonders" and "Beauty Emergency" in *Drunken Boat*

"Answer Me This" in *Earth First News*

"The Strange Guest" and "Chinese New Year" in *Cezanne's Carrot*

"On the Beatific Rag" and "Famous Kisses" in *the eleventh muse*

"My Day the Day Allen Ginsberg Died" in *Sin Fronteras*

"Fritz Scholder" in Miriam Sagan's article on Ekphrasis in *Writer's Digest*

"On the Road in Green" in *The Harwood Review*

"Concert" in *Harwood Anthology*

"Pittsburgh Encore" in *Looking Back to Place*, Old School Books

"The Persian Bride" (now titled "The Strange Guest") and "Prayer Flags" in *Intimate Witness*, a video by Video Magic

"Birth Song" in *Black Bear Review*

"Singing Down" in *Mothering Magazine*

"Ghazal in B" (now titled "October Eros in B") and "Ghazal for Blood Oranges" in *Ghazal Pages*

"How to Get to My House" and "True or False" in *Santa Fe Literary Review* 2005 and 2009

"How I Got Here" in *We Came to Santa Fe*, Pennywhistle Press, 2009

Museum pieces "Talpa Winter: by Andrew Dasburg," "The Pull North," and "Fritz Scholder" were written for the Museum of New Mexico's 85th anniversary and taped at a public celebration to be played alongside works of art in the Museum, 2002–2003

"Famous Kisses" in *Taos Poetry Circus: The Nineties*, written and edited by Anne MacNaughton with Peter Rabbit, Amalio Madueño, and Terry Jacobus, Pennywhistle Press

"What Caught My Eye" in *El Palacio Magazine* from the Museum of New Mexico

"Fritz Scholder" in *Writer's Digest*"

PERMISSIONS: Thanks to Peter Levitt for his poem from *One Hundred Butterflies*, Broken Moon Press, May 1992.

What I Learned in the Dark

❧

. . . dark, too, blooms and sings
—Wendell Berry, "To Know the Dark"

On My 60th

Sunday after the all night drive
Hailstorms and we're packing for a trip
Everyone you love will surely die

I'm turning sixty, melons on the vine
I navigate my life, a stunning blip,
Monday morning before the all day drive.

You say I'm morbid, where's the blooming lie?
Shall I let my oldest secrets slip?
Everyone I love will someday die.

Before our excursion to the skies
Nobody's about to give me lip
Tuesday morning, we're all packed to fly.

Feisty conclusion, no more "I."
Heaven and hell are joined at the hip
Everyone we hold will let go, die.

Please be here, my darling, my blue eye
You and I once separate, old and hip,
Wednesday morning, counting, days go by
Everyone you love will (gently or raging) die.

What I Learned in the Dark

A horse talked to me in my sleep.
He was an ally, and advocate.
He was my lawyer, defending me
From mediocre and slothful ways.

He said, *learn from the dark.*
To be a black horse is one kind
Of camouflage, to be roan is another.
You think it's a breeze being a horse

Because we sleep standing up
Or that's what they say. Actually
We stand in attention to dreams.
We list and sway microscopically.

I have a large vocabulary for a horse,
I know, but that's because you're listening.

The other night my old friend said
As she drove away in a truck bristling
With branches and litter, *You should*
probably leave.

The next day she called
on the telephone, told me life was a mess.
Marriage could end, a house bend
A couple in four ways.

The lunatic wind of spring by day.
In the dark I mend slowly. He reaches
For my sacrum, hand like an awl,
Hand like Christ, hand like a sun

On my back, hand like Lord Krishna
On the flute, hand like a thug, granary
Hand, farmer hand on the small
Of the back and I learned that love

Resides more in flesh than in word
And I already know there is no death.
I learned contradiction, the body
Brings me to what is eternal

Even as I run down. In the dark we wrestle
Motives and wring out problems,

Unsolvable lovable dark. Daylight
Is a solvent for black. It dilutes worry.
I drink the tiny-leafed tea from Kenya
So fine it can't be strained, must settle.

Each time I make a cup I think of AIDS.
Each physical thing is a stand-in for God.

I love the stand-up comedians of daylight.
A robin, an eighth grade boy at the Indian
School, *Just Kidding*, he says, *just kidding*.
"I kid you not!" my eighth grade teacher

used to say. Every right can be turned
inside out to a wrong. My daughter, Hope,
has darkness and radiance, like those clouds
with beams we call Hallelujah chorus.

I'm open to learn, dear dark.
Have your way with me.

Daybreak

Daybreak appears
When a horse neighs
—Teton Sioux, translated by Frances Densmore, 1918

When the five men died I fell
Into a deep sleep. I woke in 1998.
I woke in 2003. I woke today, every
Morning with its tribal forgiveness.

Each day the fight of the night
Before forgiven. Morning
Carries a *Get Out of Jail Free* card.
Houdini morning, escape from water.

Morning with its attendant odes
And aubades, its acolytes. He is never
Mad at me. My mother forgave me
For hating her over contorted issues.

A pink purse with a red dress. Permanent
Waves. Morning, my Buddha, Quan Yin.
Morning who hears the cries of the world.
We have one wren, one mockingbird.

Let go from the get go. By now the wolves
Are calling the coyotes to casinos.
I drove past the hunch of fur feeding
By Camel Rock. I sped by but the curve stayed.

I drink only tea. That was lovely, tea
Says in a snooty accent. Even the worst
Dreams release me. You love me.
Death will be a morning.

February 4th

The slow world never caught me.
I held every sorrow at bay for a week,
the villagers and rice, the saddest
astronaut, the afterthought

of Agent Orange left on the returned.
I held Mercy on my lap, child one,
child two, and by the third child I came out
and named her Hope, called it by name.

The veil of ash and hatred parts
when your water breaks, labors till
a head, a head, holy kingdom
of tectonic plates and celestial wiring.

Minute universe cutting swaths of breath
through the world, all the women breathing
and the teary-eyed men. The centuries
line up, Moses, Jesus, Mohammed, Buddha,

and our lives make replications of the holy,
knockoffs but the same perfume of God.
The slow Universe breathes relief, asks Peace
of us. How can we refuse?

Inviting the Elephant into the Room

Let's say you meet someone
whose grief is more than anyone can bear.
They have lost a beloved son, a country,
a war, an entire family, an earth, garden
of thoughts. Let's say they are sitting
across from you at dinner, or cannot eat,
but the elephant of their grief is weighing
down the room or the century or blighting
the roses, let's just say.

There is nothing
you can pour into their wounds,
no salt can bring more sting, no paper
can cover the rock, no scissors cut the cord
of attachment to their loss. You know
you could be them one day, will be, are them,
were them, if you are truly able
to love and carry the full bore of your loving.

You want to help. Somehow, but let's just say
this person, this planet, is beyond reaching.
No triage, no effort can staunch the flow.
You find yourself swiveling on your chair,
turn to the screen, YouTube, and in Thailand
an elephant takes up a paintbrush

paints a self-portrait, not of heaviness
but of grace, light on her feet, trunk able
to retrace and darken delicate lines.
And for five minutes you all stare at a thing
beyond human and then with a flourish
the elephant adds a flower in her trunk's
grasp. You all gasp and as if dancing
could occur, were already occurring, applause,
a pause just long enough for the tip of beauty
to insert its foot into the door of sadness
and you make those sounds, of pleasure.
Let's just say this is being alive.

All My Relations

With thanks to Christopher Smart

I'd like to consider my marriage
For it is a vessel that never poured me out
But contained me. For it has kept me off the streets
And allowed me into the synagogues
For it gave me three children and more blessing
Than money. For it lasted against odds and bad tempers.
For it is bigger than the two small operators
Pushing and pulling like bucksaw through tree.
For it has ten hands and ten feet, a hundred toes.
For it has a studious Adam and a fractious Eve.
For it has digested thirty thousand meals
And slept in proximity eleven thousand nights.

I want to consider divorce
Which delivers the subject from the object.
For bringing solitude back to the besieged.
For crafting two wholes out of two halves
For making possible a next love
For the vials of tear as precious as the ambergris of whales
For the temptation to shout divorce at minor altercations
For divorce brought my mother to my father
And their love begot me and for this
I must praise divorce.

And I want to consider solitude
For the celibate man I met on a hillside
His anger turned over and exhumed
For the woman who lives alone and is smiling
No one to blame. For the man who said
It is easier to be spiritual alone and then moved
In with his lover. For solitude, the woman who walks
Out alone into the desert for visions, the man
Who has to drag his reluctant self back from woods
Praise living alone, for the air in the room
When you wake is nothing but God.

Praise how we intersect. The tiny cemetery in
La Puebla with plastic flowers and boney sunsets.
Your children eating at my house, mine at yours.

The Forms That Choose Us

I live in marriage, which is a form
like sonnet or pagoda, which is a proclivity
like homosexuality except I live in marriage.
I live in a mixed marriage of a mediocre Jew
and a far gone, way lapsed Catholic and so
I live in mestizo land, not on a mesa but around

a table and on the table is a cut flower,
some spilled salt I throw over my shoulder,
salad every evening, a beer for him,
Kosher wine I tipple. I live in the sacred
terrain of Nuevo México or the Pennsylvania turnpike,
you got to pay the toll.

Marriage is sex on a good day, peace on a quiet one.
Small wars on TV screens reflecting large bedroom
wars, dumped sock drawers or underwear respectfully
hung on the line, veiled by sheets so the neighbors
won't see. He he he and she she she.
Marriage is my hallucination and my harmony.

It's half addiction and part pill, my mission
and my church. I'm the rabbi and the wife,
the better and of course the worse. "Who else
would have us?" my old friends used to joke.
Now he's dead and she's counting change.
I'm carrying a loaded purse.

I'm watching the aging in slo-mo unfold.
I live in matrimony. I give. I mostly take.
Try not to manipulate, though my hands
won't wear rings. In sickness less than health,
in making do and more debt than wealth.
In holy holy holy and books jamming on the shelf.

"I love you" means less than doing a chore.
I feed the dozen chickens, you hang the
slamming slamming slamming screen door.

True or False

I called and canceled the President.
The soldiers in Iraq are served speed and Ecstasy.
Some of them are 18. Some of them never touched drugs.

Afghan girls go to school in tents.
My mother lied to get into kindergarten.
A lizard shares my shadow.

We have three brains and two hemispheres.
Some share a brain with that lizard.
Ginger Rogers admired my eyebrows.

My husband has been faithful.
I have been faithful. The heart
Is fashioned of brightest dark and darkest dark.

All my writing is derivative. Shadows
Prefer Brie to Velveeta. A woman in Todos Santos
Named Lorna told me to grow my hair.

I have lost Lorna but took her advice.
Advice is made of advertising and vice.
Advice is a second cousin of guilt.

Cousins can marry in certain states.
The state of Maine, just wanted to say Maine.
Wallace Stevens' grandson never read his poems.

Dark chocolate is loaded with antioxidants.
You'd think antioxidants were the shrine of Mary.
A woman called me her bright shadow.

I named my last child Hope. I never had a last child.
Television is the Golden Calf I read about
In Sabbath School. My teacher lied.

We live on the northern edge of the Sonorous desert.
Armageddon is a small lizard that reconstitutes at first rain.
Turtles have an aversion to helium because they are heavyhearted.

Sigmund Freud dropped his lighter outside a Viennese brothel.
My husband found Sigmund Freud's lighter.
Starfish can regenerate one leg, but two is too many.

Star of David is a brand of tuna. Unleavened bread
Travels well on sea journeys. If you move counterclockwise
Time stretches to fit the container of a day.

I love how square his chin is, with or without a beard.
Some tarot readers are prescriptive.
Some astrologers were born under a bad sign.

Astronomy resents being called astrology and sends down
Instant karma on the one who utters the mistake.
I am so tired it almost feels good.

If I could sleep here tonight I would, in a new nightgown.
But I can't and I won't.
The oldest tree is the bristlecone pine.

The oldest man turns into a woman.
My stepfather is kind to me at 97.
I love him like I love smoked fish.

Sigmund Freud ate sushi and based
His seminal work on seaweed. The dreams
Of the skunk are pure and lyrical.

Perfumes refuse to be silenced,
Scream inside bottles. School buses
Hum in the night to get the sadness

Out of all that fake leather. My daughter
Is and is not okay. My other daughter
Is younger than she thinks. I give up,

Luckily have cowboys with bootstraps.
The arroyos are up late at night kibitzing
About when the toads will return.

More lizards with new tails cross the garden.
My lettuce is taking out a subscription
To *Organic Gardening* in hope of a better life.

Our cat is easier on the birds than you are
On me. Our grandson has excuses for everything
And he can't talk yet.

My favorite animal
Is the rotunda of the state capitol.
Every evening the blowfish play

Conch shells to lower the sun. A tambourine
Is a frame drum. Even antidepressants
Can have a bad day.

Orgasm is a kind
Of snail that lives in northern Oregon.
Carl Jung grew very old and learned to fly.

Building with adobe is less costly
Than a mobile home. My heart youngens
As I write. Blue ink lowers cholesterol.

Dialogue: Truth and Time

Time says, there is never enough of me
And truth says, the hens don't wear watches,
And when they go broody, it's all bets off.

Time says, the longer you watch me, the slower
I will become.
And truth says, to boil is human,
To fry, divine.

Time says, I am selling World Book Encyclopedias
To supplement my income this summer
And truth says, last night two rabbits were playing
And this morning, legs and a small ear in the kitchen

And time says: You never run out of me until your last drawn breath
And if you don't exhale, don't worry, I will go on breathing
Carry on without you and truth says:

Would you care for an afterdinner mint, or a small pillow
For your back. And time says:
After the mountains burn and the topsoil
Turns to glass, do clouds still matter?

Truth says, I am calling to confirm your appointment
For a truth cleaning at 11 a.m.
And time stages a walk out, carrying picket signs
To strike against its own tyranny.

And time says, the rosary is an accurate device for counting days.
And truth answers, do grace and time share a table
At the diner, a booth by a jukebox?

October Eros in B

For Agha Shahid Ali

The old beauty we love wears a gold bee on his lapel.
A stunning man died recently from the sting of a bee.

The Sicilian woman nods, twiddles her brilliant thumbs.
Even her habits are blessed choreography, the dance of bees.

How can we document happiness in a plain white life?
Hold on. If you want some sting, don't ask me, ask the bees.

You, my impossible, turn out to be my breathing Paradise.
We sit at a card table for years, dine out, shoo away bees.

My neighbor fought for England, moved here, still limps on a gimpy
British knee. Grows extravagant gardens, raises honey bees.

Agha, who taught me ghazal, has cancer. May his span of days
be filled with Urdu gardens where dragonflies dally with bees.

He said, "Guitars get jealous," tuned his to another frequency.
My son has a fretful guitar, drives east, navigating by the bees.

John Lennon dead twenty years, right when I started poetry.
His killer's parole denied, as if Mother Mary piped up, "Let it be."

I made a lunch date Yom Kippur when I needed to stay empty.
Extenuating circumstances of love, Book of Life, let me be.

To be or not to be was the old question. Nowadays old
Joan Logghe is strangely vain. She thinks she's the queen bee.

Good Investments

Is this a maple tree's sap
Or an injured boy from Vermont home from the war?

Is this an interpretation of dreams
Of Freud's suspenders found under his desk?

Is this the way water mixes with clouds
And you drink beer anyway?

Is this a flirtation of sparrows or some leftover
Starlings after the girl shoots them with her grandpa's gun?

Is this a good investment in sagebrush
Or the cactus thorns that adorn the latest saint?

Is this the beginning of a marriage
Or the execution of lilacs?

Is the name more important than the face?
Why are surnames lined up to enlist in the army?

Is the bombing of seventeen Pakistanis worth
The price of a missed terrorist?

Who established the ring as a symbol for weddings?
Why not give each other rice crackers?

Are lunatics all women because they ride bicycles
And roulette wheels home from the soup kitchen?

Who christens the casinos with the back taxes
Of lost houses?

Are gamblers all optimists? Do pessimists
Make better mothers?

Can Joan Logghe learn Spanish
When Hebrew words clog her memory?

Ghazal for a Young Married Zen Student

You are not living in ancient times.
You are not living in modern times, only in time.

This is an arranged marriage. Remember
emptiness gave you each other for a time.

Years you might be civil, polite, and kind
and then you need the feral darkness of crazy time.

Nothing is personal, love is blind, death is sure.
Do you wish you could be courteous all the time?

You should get divorced. Immediately. Right now.
Get married a little later, tonight, next week, you'll know the time.

The number of sentient marriages is endless.
I vow to save them all, but can't all the time.

Do you know that old country song, our affluent anthem?
"If you've got the money, honey, I've got the time."

Reduced to silence in the arms of the mystery,
where is my wise woman when I need her this time?

Take weeks apart, walk in opposite directions, then run,
arms open, shouting in the park, "It was you all the time."

How can I offer advice when I've bumbled and flailed?
I dwell in holy confusion for the sake of deep time.

Radiant daughter of form and formlessness,
Joan Logghe says, *Take your time.*

War Time

After the Talking Heads spoke of war
I made pancakes with very high cholesterol
my secret recipe, adding blue cornmeal
so it wouldn't be a total loss, thought
of my husband at a wedding in Santa Barbara
saint of fire and wondered what I was the saint
of. Matron saint of worry I said last night
as a drunk Republican said a dozen times
"A billion dollars. Put a bounty on Osama
for a billion dollars." I became right wing,
we need both wings these days, there by the bonfire
for an old friend off to Kenya for the Peace Corps
her two store cakes said WORLD PEACE in frosting.
The drummers from Nigeria so sweet I finally cried.

I ate red, white, and blue M&Ms all week watching
the horrible news. I had picked them up on sale
at Walmart superstore where I could buy live lobsters
and old Santa Clara pueblo women walked with small
steps behind their carts in some old woman amazement
at the kinds of shampoo. I bought the cheapest kind,
but still take my vitamins. My hair may go to hell
before I do. Today the thunder is so loud, you know
what it reminds me of. I rolled pennies on Thursday
and my daughter asked how many. Fifteen dollars
I said. 1,500 bodies she thought and told me later.
They were heavy in my hands as copper grief.
My daughter studies chemistry tonight so very long.

Be tender. Bathe often. Watch that praying mantis
flying around our living room, maybe on patrol
for her mate, the one we stepped on accidentally last week.
Though they eat their mates, don't they?
I swear I will lay off my husband for his new love
of cigarettes. Pretend he is a fellow at a bar.
It's wartime. We only have this once.

Sitting Shivah for Iraq: 3/30/03 *

I am sitting *shivah* for Iraq
The city of Baghdad which I'll never see
Which no one can ever see who has not already seen it.

We cover the mirrors, we sit close to the ground,
We tear our garments like any woman would.
When I hear the words Tigris and Euphrates
A small woman inside me tears her robes
Covers her mirror which is an old river.

Did I hear the word *cradle*? The two rivers converge
To shape a womb where Inanna was born.
I am sitting *shivah* for innocence. My daughter has lived
Between Gulf War and Gulf War. Her favorite peace
Sign is "And they say they're Pro-life."

Our baby knocks over his blocks and laughs
When the towers fall, innocent with perfect glee.
But my mind scrambles glee into uniform.

I am sitting *shivah* even as I walk through day.
We cover the mirrors, we stay close to the ground,
We eat an egg, hard-boiled, return to life.

* *Shivah* is the traditional seven-day period of Jewish mourning that begins after the funeral in the home of the deceased.

Going Ahead

Since all is behind me I'm going ahead
to the next death, the next lovemaking.

I'm going to days when nothing noteworthy
occurs, when I do no harm.

I'm going to sweet and to sour,
to egg rolls and to gin. With ten fingers

I'm going to my hands and using them
for prayer, which is to assemble a meal

made out of dead birds and rice.
With two feet I'm encouraging my legs

to walk and with two hearts, my belly
to love. Since all is ahead I'm going

into my past. Sending e-mail to the first man
I loved as a volcano loves an island, as a mushroom

loves a dead tree, as a holocaust needs
its victims. I am reaching into my mother

and pulling out pin curls and nail polish bottles
to make her an assemblage of her past.

I am cutting out photos of my favorite dead
and making a collage so I can burn with them.

We are all paper. We are scissors.
We are rock and match.

Since I think in lines, I will eat only circles,
oranges, Life Savers, tangelos, and eggs.

I will give myself lovers in every shape,
now an Appaloosa, now a thornbush with berries.

And I am going to burn, going to die
with only a contrail of words and work.

I am going to establish no state or municipalities.
Will it be simple? You tell me.

I know that it will move and change,
which means monsoon, monastery, accordion,

weight lifter, frenzy, asteroid, maniac,
kickboxing, appetite, tattoo.

I am going ballistic, going postal, gone
fishing. Would you like to accompany me?

Darling, would you like to come along
anytime soon?

Ghazal for Blood Oranges

For Marc Ellis

The sliced moon clutches the sky like a segment of blood orange.
Her Catholic husband reminds her what it means to be a Jew.

It is at moonrise the fear grows wild, men throwing
rocks, how can the men throwing gunfire be Jews?

Two extremes. Where are the quiet voices, the mothers, the lovers,
peaceable kingdom of Arab lambs lying down next to lion Jews?

Put this in the hands of women, the Arab journalist says
about his people and the Jews.

Fingers on the left hand, fingers on the right,
"Cousins," Naomi said of the Arabs and the Jews.

In October, during war times, Naomi and I stripped and soaked
among women who could not tell a naked Arab from a Jew.

Living so far out she raised her children with no affiliation,
weeps when she sits in her childhood temple, east among Jews.

Daughters of Jerusalem, I was the daughter of a haberdasher
now buried on a steep hillside filled with Russian Jews.

I dream of the city of Jerusalem, the blood orange
one fruit of God filled with sections of Arabs and Jews.

We have been whipping this camel a thousand years.
Isn't it time to bite a date, break bread, transcend Arab and Jew?

An eye for an eye, an UZI for a rock. The late poet Amichai said,
"If we're always right, spring never comes," and he was a Jew.

I have apologized, stood tall in public. My hands
have thrown stones. My hands have held guns aimed at Jews.

I'd have been lousy in the holocaust, no Anne Frank.
If I were Israeli now, what kind of Jew?

My Zen teacher travels to Auschwitz. The sons
of Nazi guards sit next to the daughters of old Jews.

Bismillah or *S'hema*. We are the Arab son killed in his father's arms.
We are the guns. Listen, God wrestlers, isn't God One?

Lorca at the Bosque del Apache*

The snow geese were there all along
Making their artificial snow.
The grebes were filing a grievance.
There were thirty some thousand geese
And eight plus thousand cranes
But who was counting?

Lorca was, the hours after his death were
Increasing like flocks.

My grandson said his body ached,
He felt all flocked out.
In my dreams there were caves and mud plaster
Everything became suddenly easy.
I give up several times a week.
Lorca reminds me I have bootstraps.
I miss Lorca as if we were in relationship.
There are five other men I miss, not counting
My father, but who's counting?

Right now the whole
Country, three plus thousand soldiers gone.
Right now the 3 a.m. train is whistling through San Antonio.
My grandson is asleep in Glorieta.
The snow geese are asleep without lullabyes.
I met Madeline at the Flight Deck.
She smiled sweetly as if she loved me.

When one is in the presence of cranes and geese
I defy you not to love.

* The Bosque is a bird sanctuary in San Antonio, New Mexico, along the Rio Grande.
During winter months huge flocks gather there, to fly in at dusk and out at dawn.

The train is closer now and loud.
I am listing towards a morning when the fly-out occurs.
Lorca tells me to sleep in, that morning is overrated.
The words *polar bear* are in the endangered word list.
This rattle. This raucus. The bus in Burque said $OUCH!
I am trying to interpret buses. I read the geese
Like tea leaves but they are cross-stitching the sky.
The skeins of geese and cranes,
The skeins. . . .
Of geese and cranes, the skeins.

Love, That Thread We Hang By

꧁

*I'll be so busy counting my blessings, when I die
I won't even notice it.*
—Francis Ford Coppola on *The Tavis Smiley Show*

Love, That Thread We Hang By

I.

This morning, taking my usual exit to Santa Fe
By the De Vargas Mall, I saw a man in a black suit
Walking the ramp next to a woman in shorts.
I wanted to give them a ride.

Was he carrying other clothes on a
Hanger, was he a groom?
Why was she tattooed and why didn't they get
Along very well now that it was hot? I saw a woman

Smiling in her car, then another couple, he
With a Mohawk and holding hands with her
As they crossed Paseo de Peralta, she had her chin
Upturned in pride it seemed at their coupleness,

In being with the young muscle of a man
And her face like a horse in rut, some old
Sexual gesture one doesn't see anymore, I saw.
Only then was the world illuminated oddly and slowly,
I'm still making the curve onto Guadalupe Street
And at the Lota Burger the people waiting
For their number to be called stand as if placed

And there is a dog, I'm sure his tail is curled to the left,
And it all stands almost still. I think, this is it.
This is the message to go slowly. I felt death
To be near, an encoded light you can't ask for and get.
Lucky and scared. Blessed and carefully I drove
Towards the bank to deposit what time I have left.

II.

Don't let me forget to tell you about yesterday, how a couple
married thirty-five years felt so lucky and so tired
That they didn't talk at dinner, how he read
And she watched the plants grow darker in August.
The Anniversary gifts they exchanged were so simple
And necessary, two pairs of Levis for him, a clutch
Of falling apart roses for her, as if they gave each of them
Themselves, one sturdy worthiness and one blowsy

Extravagance picked at a neighbor's. They went to a movie,
Held hands, talked to another couple they knew
At the Dreamcatcher Cinema south of Española.
The curses and blessings lie down next to each other,
In rows like clacking dominos, crows lined up,
Or bolts of fabric. Their life is both rusted and tasty.
They are both bored and engaged. They have given up
And not lost hope. Two ambiguous darlings, these two
On an August night when the spiders are sure
They'll be called for jury duty, and the crows are the judges.
Some say, *Guilty, guilty, guilty*. Little birds sing, *forgive.*
Forgive.

III.

She read Antonio Machado to me
As if I'd never heard the poem.
As if he were not my uncle,

Not my other husband, as if we had
Never met, as if the garden I am trying

To resurrect from hopeless hooligan
And cruel mess is not symbiotic and emblematic.
One gardener said, *I hate thorns,*
Nothing with thorns, and I tried to live that way.

But my teacher gave me thorns, said to me, *Dear
Joan, it's all Roses and Thorns, roses and thorns.*
And a little medal of St. Lucy I carry with me to this day.

How are you, dear teacher, living in Woodstock, New York,
With your birds wearing black as you do?
I have found a gardener who herself has tasted blood.

How are you, Machado, dead in Civil War? You carried
Your mother out on your lap, you carried the thorns of birdsong,
The roses of poems that curled on the paper in your valise.

The crows are going ballistic tonight.
They must be onto me. They must
Know something or else why are they informing

On Machado, on the wasted gardens and
The tended ones, on the odor that comes
Before rain?

IV.
The mother I am uses a broom.
Uses a green corrugated washrag.
Runs a sponge. Pulls sheet taut.
The one I am not dines alone
Eavesdropping on Japanese waiters.
Buys an extra pen for lucky.

The mother I am not. Oh, my grandchildren
Are pulling on my braids. Oh, I must not be afraid
To be happy. Oh, I have to stand for this life

And know others have harder lives and no one
Has an easy one. One friend had money
And she drowned. One friend said to me,
*Mudhita is a Buddhist precept to rejoice
in the happiness of others.* As much as compassion
Asks that we partake in the pain, but not swallow it whole.
Those crows tonight are digesting pain and song.
Their band plays a free concert on Acequia Madre,
Mother Ditch, hold enough water for this century.

V.
I can't mention a body without mentioning
Death, and I cannot say *death* without recalling
The birth of my daughter, first child and then

I can't mention her without thinking of peach blossoms
And bones, and I can't think of peaches and bones
And not mention stones and calcium, without thinking

Of stupidity and teeth, and that leads me to war
And the next moment is television and soldiers,
Which brings me immediately to prayer and my son

On September 11, the urge to enlist, and September was right
When my mother died and my mother's death was just
Inside of a good dream and you know how dreams

Come out of the body and how in the morning
They can live or they may die.

VI.

Being alive knocks me out.
It gets pricier, this life, it gets sweeter.
I recall Adeline, oldest woman
In our belly dance class, who said
As the grief gets deeper so does
Her happiness. Her hair white
As mine. I conceived a son that night.
He is a father now and a groom.
I was knocked up by love.

VII.

Care for your friends and the kids
But retain your solitude.

When you met him you lived alone.
Both of you a force.

Lake Michigan down the block,
He jumped in in winter.

, Then the fish washed up in spring.
You drank wine with a cat on the bottle.

Dear Innocent Ones, you didn't know
You'd go into hell.

You didn't know you'd put all your effort,
Your best pains, to make your choosing

Each other be right. No one can tell
If you were meant for this.

You grabbed a hand as you'd grab an oar
When you wanted to return from a cold lake.

VIII.

We're both two ways, conscious and unconscious
Every day we move toward each other

With beautiful conscious eyes
And giants throw logs under our feet.

Tricksters stage guerilla warfare
On our sanity. Little critics write scathing reviews.

Yet for some unrepentant moment,
Some bourgeois impresario of an instant,

I choose unconsciously, in half tones,
To consciously stay by you.

Nothing but Opening

The pot I am burnishing
has no handles, nothing
but opening and vessel.

Like Kabir's jug which held
stars and mountains, this clay
comes from above and below

and holds water on the head
of a Pueblo woman forty years ago
coming from the River of Roses

which is my mind. Pot. River. Woman.
Roses. And silence which is forty silences
and the tears forty lives deep.

Such a Pretty Baby, Such a Catastrophe

Such sweet thoughts at a dire moment,
Such green and I have never seen jungle,
Such and so was saying today, on the streets of Pittsburgh
Oliver Avenue, Grant Avenue with its courthouse,
Liberty with the Army/Navy Surplus store.

Such nostalgia one feels for the vapors of steel mills.
Such a long time ago I sat in the Ellsworth back yard.
Such invasions into my dreaming, the hedge
Between families creating a long panorama
Of urban space, such as my mother waking cheerfully
To my dour girl. Such as the country club which
Haunts me like an affluent ghost, laugh at my failures,

Such as the day I made them finally proud
But my father was already dead, such as definitions
Of success I scouted for ethics class from Rodef Shalom
Synagogue where I found my own scales of justice,
Such as Baruch Atah Adonai, Blessed art Thou
Oh Lord, such as a day encrusted with ice.
I was going to say blessing but ice is the truth.

Such as the crush of the shoe against solid
Patch of water, the pleasure of crunch,
The satisfaction of each step, such as the approach
Of a jet to a runway, each landing miraculous,
Such as my husband saying traffic alone is proof
Of God and I think of that, keeping spaces
Between cars sacred, such as our argument
About hope or imagination, his latest trip.

Such as words we used when we met in 1969,
Trip, far out, righteous, stoned, mellow, in each
Word I am wearing that coral batik shirt I wish
I'd never sold, such as a thought with no conclusion,
A breath with an open end, do we die on an inhale
Or an exhalation such as the day I walked across
The room holding *Tender is the Night*, age 21, age 58,

Such as it is and was always meant to be, suchness
The Buddhists say. Such jewels.

All of the Sudden

*The moment I saw the brilliant, proud morning shine high up over the
deserts of Santa Fe, something stood still in my soul, and I started to attend.*
—D. H. Lawrence

Only this morning, a Sabbath in February
waking from a dream of robbing the blind
woman's cabin, using her oils, sanding a casket

and sharpening her small saws.
She forgives everything. All of the worry gone,
all of a sudden that blasted anguish at rest.

Anxiety, my friend and I laugh on the phone,
at bay. The evil eye blinked closed. My own
evil twin of hand-wringing at rest. I woke elated.

Could it be because my cousin sent me photos
of my grandmother cut in black ink, body
I'd never seen with her white hair and thick ankles?

Woman I never knew, car accident young.
Could it be her prayers too, at very least
her good thick-ankle genes hold me

who got to live after the war. 1930s, 1942
the photos date. Woman Born After the War.
Or held in the nets of ancestral prayer.

I had to get out of my bed and my ease,
away from the good warmth of a good man,
to get this down. Document happiness before it passes.

On other mornings, dark as they may come,
I will hold my hands to this and warm them
on today's small fire. Let it be known

that on the earth there dwelled a happy woman,
blessed in every way, knock wood. Even then
she forgot and forgot.

It took many women touching her
on the eyes and took her touching back,
for her to risk and see.

My Mother's Heart

My mother's heart saved money to go to college and become a teacher
My mother's heart lost all her money in the Crash
My mother's heart went to beauty college, owned a salon
My mother's heart planned the menus but never cooked
My mother's heart ate ice cream, Rocky Road
My mother's heart flew to Florida in 1959 and got a hole-in-one
My mother's heart learned Italian to keep her mind active
My mother's heart was one of the ten best dressed hearts in Pittsburgh
My mother's heart ate Chinese food at the Tea Garden
My mother's heart opened a charge account at Kaufman's,
   gave me the card
My mother's heart had room for one son, one daughter
And then we multiplied like the Old Testament and her heart kept up
My mother's heart cried when she lit candles on Friday night
My mother's heart is singing, "I'm gonna live till I die.
I'm gonna laugh till I cry."
My mother's heart was a honeycomb fed by the bees of commerce
My mother's heart is the apple of my eye, the cat's pajamas,
the bee's knees
My mother's famous heart is giving to charity, volunteering at day care
at the Jewish Home for the Aged
My mother's retired heart played bridge,
shopped with coupons, kept her night vision and drove her car fast
My mother's final heart is watching *Who Wants to be a Millionaire*
night after night

My mother's ocean heart sits out on the balcony for the oxygen that
comes off the Atlantic. I want to drop everything right now and praise
my mother's heart. I want to fall on my knees and rejoice in such a
mother. I want to forgive the old patriarchy because a woman like my
mother rose out of it, despite all opposition. One generation out of the
Old Country, my mother's New World pure 100 percent Hungarian
heart.

The Seven Wonders

Finally, a truck drives into my heart
With its massive tires and leaves my heart
An occupied destination, a motor club Triptych to Alive.
The scenic route or the freeway, no matter, we finally arrive,
Get to the heart, pitch our tent, quarrel because
We always do when we drive those stakes, hungry, sing
Because we have to, go swimming in the heart, wash
Our hands and linger there though we smell the pigs
From the feedlots down the road. Wish we had made
This trip sooner, I say to no one in particular
And to our youngest child who is taking hurdles,
Winning a medal. I say to my mother, whose heart
Is a sputtering vehicle on the beach, "How come
Nobody drove into my heart before? Wasn't the rate
Decent? Weren't the views all along spectacular?
Isn't the restaurant four stars, the sheets clean?"
The seven wonders of the invisible woman in the
Hidden indivisible world.

Beauty Emergency

1. Out beyond permanent waves there is a field.
My mother lives there, Queen of the Day.
Take a disposable camera of your mother's last year.
In the pool she let me go, saying, *Swim!*

Her final year in Pittsburgh, Boca Raton.
Dark nights of the soul are not for her, she's blond.
In the pool she let me go, moving back, saying *Swim!*
Out of your life doing the Jewish Lady Crawl.

Dark nights of the soul are not for her, she's blond.
The Hungarian Revolution made her weep. After
All her life she never did the Jewish Lady Crawl
To save her hair, for she was the Queen of Beauty.

The Hungarians made her weepy. After all
She needs help to walk, here comes the bride, Miss Third Street
Save her here, who is the actual Aphrodite.
In case of a medical Emergency Do Not Call 911.

Here comes the bride in a wheelchair, Miss Third Street.
In case of a beauty emergency call 911.
In case of a medical emergency do not panic.
Cry out, *Shema, Listen, God is everywhere.*

2. In case of a beauty emergency do not panic.
Write down each conversation as if it were the last.
Say the Shema, Listen, God is one
Way or another, we all go back to God.

Write down each conversation.
"I wear lipstick, don't I?"
One way or another we all go back to God,
In biblical begets, back to the strong ones.

She said on Rosh Hashanah, "I wear lipstick, don't I?"
My brother is my guru, holy man of cell phone.
The biblical begets back to the godly.
She lives on oxygen between bed and couch and table.

My brother is my guru, the good man does exist.
In sacred geometry, she dwells between three places
On oxygen between bedroom, couch and table.
She is so small, but loves so hugely.

In sacred geometry she dwells between three worlds.
Take a disposable camera of her last days.
She is so small but loves so hugely.
Out beyond permanent waves, there is a field.

Viva Beauty

Every morning it sounds like thanks,
The light, those birds on the maple.
My mother alive one day
One day not.

I have a friend who knows how
To make me smile. I have a husband
Who drives me wild both ways
And so, long life is good.

I wrote my mother when I wakened
About the afterlife. As if I were the rabbi,
As if I saw the ocean. I remind her the ocean
Is full of tears and laughter.

I tell her the morning
Is for gratitude. No, I am confused
She's telling me, "Once you have tankas
In your blood, you're free to write sambas."

My mother is still teaching me
Though she finally stopped trying.
Have I told you, I'm half Hungarian?
And my half brother is all Hungarian.

My mother always said *Men, typical,*
Typical men liked to be waited on
And it's our fault. My brother proves
How right a man can act. Sweetening the end.

My mother changed the world.
She rose up like the sun over the Atlantic.
She gave money, worked six days a week.
I knew a woman always blond.

Now she is breathing hard. All gratitude
Going back to the birds who first praised,
My mother came out of me and I
Out of her. The sky can sweeten.

I don't care how rotten I was as a girl.
I have sweetened. Those who run
The world on cogs and gears can change
Their ways too. By my mother's decree.

Evanescence

For Hope

I want to give you a word,
evanescent, because your vocabulary
for grief is being forced wider.

I could come up with more useful words,
rubbery and dull. *Lamentable*
comes to mind.

But I crave gifts this week
in the wake of the death
of your friend Raven's boyfriend.

Eli, the beautiful lost in the beautiful.
Evanescent. A word Emily Dickinson
favored, as she did *transmogrify*.

What a year: two grandmas, Twin Towers,
my friend in the Rio Grande, now this.
So I offer a word for dragonflies

and all things vaporous and tending
to vanish. My mother never needed
this word her whole life.

She had Hungarian and the Great
Depression. She said, "Thank you
sweetheart," in Hungarian every day.

You need this word, fleeting
in your brevity and shimmer,
you with your sixteen summer beauty.

In the wake of College Board scores,
iridescence, running hurdles, all of it,
evanescence comes along.

Here, take this world
and make the most of it.

Daughter Running
In the style of André Breton

My daughter whose face is a face of sooner not late
My daughter with a graduating heart and a mind finally at ease,
With a focus made of monograms and health,
Whose eyes can't get enough of foreign lands
Whose eyes have seen the sky and spoken Spanish to it
Whose Spanish-speaking eyes plead for independence
My daughter whose hazel eyes change like calendars
Whose eyes never reminisce and rarely cry
Who looks ahead like a joyful singing clock
My daughter at eighteen with a voter's booth inside
And a vote cast for peace, whose reggae hips
Are marimbas of constancy. Whose Bob Marley heart
Is a heart of flame. My daughter who is moving from home
Who can't wait to evacuate the sinking elder ship
My daughter who is flying to Santa Cruz, holy saint
Of Española in a joke, who is falling into college
Like into leaves. Where jade plants the size of cars
And hen and chicks as big as serving plates await.
My daughter who is renting a terrarium and living
Under ferns, sleeping on moss.
My avocado branch, my chai, my Cheerio
My California-ready daughter, my cutting teeth
On love daughter, my only child at home already
Gone. My youngest one with a hat of empty nest.
My evacuation plan daughter, my heart at free fall,
My daughter whose poetry jumps hurdles over mine.
My surrender girl, my homework looming daughter
Driving far to school. Thanks to the holy universe
For assembling parts as wildly lovely as these.

Holy Cool

That one summer she said it was "cool,"
Every other word at summer camp in the Jemez
And all, even with the fires heading close and fast
Cool the boys and cool the guitars and it was awfully
Cool as the fire engulfed 47,000 acres heading
Toward the plutonium stored above ground, cool
That the firefighters fought all night only three
Years ago and she was fifteen, we evacuated
For her birthday and it is cool now she's turned
Eighteen and moved out of the house this week
Onto Apache St. past Blockbuster Video and into
The grunge of city summer, no money, no fans
Or air conditioning, the Great Books on a shelf
But I'm cool so I deliver eggs from our sacred chickens
And she's coolly camping at Santa Barbara
And I'm pretty cool but had no idea
Where she was and how she found a black
Boyfriend in Santa Fe, but I'm cool with that
It's not like she was dating a Right Winger
And everybody seems to know his father
As far north as Taos so he must be cool.
Both of my daughters like gaps in teeth
It must be cool though I paid an orthodontist
Enough to put a car in their mouths.
The policeman called, he was pretty cool
Considering he found her underwear and
Personal effects on the corner of Apache
And Hopi after her car was robbed & I
Have been relatively cool though she rarely
Calls, giving me practice in leaving before
She leaves, cool huh? Like five years ago
When he gave me rehearsals of pain so
I'd disentangle my sinew from his leg muscle
And get a life which I thought I had but

I was pretty uncool until now I have gotten
A good deal cooler in the heart. I'm chill.
I'm still from Pittsburgh but New Mexico
Is my cool factory. Just living here
Gives me a sort of card-carrying coolness.

My Blue Heaven

And baby makes three, we're happy
(in my green heaven, turpentine and jade,
tourmaline, the smell of Pine-Sol
and green beans. My yellow heaven,
lemon Jell-O and Murphy's Oil Soap,
bananas and twisted hemp, aspen
and my red heaven in blood times,
maraschino cherries and lists
with red balances and cliffs streaked
with iron and my silver heaven,
rings and change and rain clouds,
and sequins and chrome car parts.
My datura heaven, white bread and delusion
and insomnia and near death experience,
My black heaven, heaving the coal into the
shuttle at the moment of actual death
and my Robert, my Don, my Harry, dark
bearded ones. On purpose, you did it,
my blame heaven. Or roses and roses
and pink babies from pink people,
my Caucasian heaven and my interracial
heaven. My stir-fry heaven of shrimp,
camarones, my Spanish heaven,
boracho and *linda*, and my Persian heaven,
miniatures and my stereotypical heaven
where everyone always does as expected)
in my blue heaven.

My Day the Day Allen Ginsberg Died

I was reading *White Shroud* in bed at 5 a.m.,
angry at everything, have to get up too early,
I'm not in the mood to drive south.

Last night at a party a man stripped
to display his Krishna and Buddha tattoos
over sagging chest flesh. Ginsberg says

"I am summoned from my bed
to the Great City of the Dead." I
don't want to drive to Albuquerque,

am transfixed by the old bag of breath
my professor of way gay Beat fame.
Cannot get enough of him, sing

"Do the Meditation Rock" under my breath.
Drag myself from words into the early
snowy, blossoming April day. Passing casinos

the day is shallow and motherly as many
of my days turn out instead of in. But Allen
is already dead and I have no idea. At YesterDave's

eat burgers, drink shakes, see Elvis's leather jacket
and his Cadillac, while Allen is no longer
breathing except this humming in me,

"Do the meditation, do the meditation."
I am poet all day secretly. Make small talk.
Buy sandals for my child, this double life I love.

A rumor reaches me, the Great
Ginsberg is dead. I missed all seventy of his
birthdays, but he gave a little birth to me, back in Boston

in the sixties. I try and watch TV. Snooze off, but wake
carrying the uncertain but urgent pregnancy of death.
On page 3 of the *Journal* two columns I skim.

I already know what it says.
Allen Ginsberg is not dead but humming
me to work. We all have more to do.

My darlings are thumbing rides to the Great
City of the Dead. Ginsberg chants the sights.
His is a breath so long it is heard from the Other Side.

I am not genius. Am mother with habit
for words after thought, when the dishwasher purrs,
the man snores, the radio speaks Spanish.

Tumbleweed flies kite-high and crazy over the house.
I am singing Ginsberg as he sang me Blake
in the seventies in San Francisco, "All the hills

echo-ed." Sang me high into the men's bathroom
at the Family Dog where the Angels of Light in
chorus girl drag showed a leg. I peed among men

dressed as women, and I write among women now,
my own live song mourns and my dervish breath
turns, saddens, and longs.

Beat Elegy

Allen Ginsberg gone, writing from "Howl"
to "Gone." Voice, *la sirena*, a gong.

The pitcher of dreams pours into me.
Allen becomes "Kaddish," blessed be he.

I receive the grace of a graceful mind,
old rabbi, old literate bell.

Allen Ginsberg is gone, catching a fish
in the om-ing Hindu sea. Playing a Sanskrit harp

at Tompkins Square Park in the Village, chanting *Hare Hare*
in 1963. I hear him there in the buzzing days

leaping like the haiku frog into the pond of me.
I see him singing in 1970 at the Family Dog.

Old *diablito*, old angel throat. Seducer of young
men to picnic under the family tree.

Feasting on storks and wine, enter a sunflower
and come out Blake. Taker of psilocybin

grass, and LSD. Under the influence of Buddhist
text and philosophy, chanter of sutras, war protests,

anti-nuclear grail. I was humming the day you died,
I didn't know you'd climbed the ladder Jacob dreamed

back to the moon for good, holy astronaut.
You called your friends to give them a Beat au revoir.

You died like a Buddhist and an old Jew,
I accept the cash you left me in your will,

a morsel of breath that has entered mine,
I can't play the violin, have no harmonium,

I was humming the day you died.
When the sky is deep with crows

and the stars meditate all night, and
my voice has a life of its own, it's Allen.

Issa's Child

Sato (1818–19)

The world of dew
Is the world of dew
and yet, and yet —
—Issa

My father loves small things
the bird, the cricket in the corner,
the moth wing

so I must leave him while I am small.
My name means "wisdom" and I know
it is my unfortunate job

to breeze in on my mother's fierce love
to breathe a while and go.
I gave one year to life.

His own mother left when he was two
and my three brothers are all fated
to lives of dragonfly's length.

That way my father, keeper of the small,
the insignificant, the low, the toad, the fly,
the swallow, the mosquito,

will be so moved all his days, that fire
for his work will feed on this sad fuel
and outlast any one body, one jot of a life.

Of Things Significant and Insignificant

Ricardo is gone, he died at 3:30, pronounced at 4:00.
The snapdragons all wilted, planted

at dusk. He left me with my work and a small daughter,
he was not mine to lose. The candlewick
from Day of the Dead is lost in wax.

Lost wax is a technique. I am not visual.
Ricardo was blind eighteen months before he died.

He was so allergic to cats it was impossible.
He is gone, taking his allergy with him.
My house was off bounds, I wondered hugging him.

I wear my cats like minks, like boas.
My mother had a stole made of mink pelts with faces.

Ricardo's mother lives an hour from my mother.
Her son is all we have in common, now nothing.
The ocean in Florida is made of amnesia.

My father met Ricardo in a speakeasy in heaven.
I send them messages from the balcony of earth.

I said the Shema inside my body beside him
silently praying. He said, "Let that be a lesson to you."
A woman held his hands, made small talk to his dying.

I am allergic to small talk, though I studied it in college.
My love for Ricardo was the lightest of loves.

My grief is almost happy, I did the heavy part
five years ago in an efficiency apartment in Deerfield
when I tossed and turned his cancer. He is okay now.

I have a happy heart. He didn't want to leave that body,
wanted to rent a car for dying. Said, "Cut me a deal."

His mother has another heart, his widow, red hair.
There are as many griefs as there are insects.
The ways of grief are limitless.

My hand covers my mouth, my now husband is breathing.
He said, "Write about this," this morning after coming.

The geraniums in our greenhouse remind me of death.
This is a long story. I can't explain it here.
I love so many dead men, have problems with the living.

The booming of car radios reminds me of angels.
There was an angel in Florida the night I mourned Ricardo.

Inside of cars is it always summer. I brace
for the next disaster, welcome the end. Instead of loss
this death has strangely filled me.

What Lovely Wine

The apples trees come in bloom. The surprised older wife
after a hundred years of hurry wears negligees
once the house is emptied. The snakes feel their way
through the grass and then it rains.
The automobile turns off. All is still.
It's as if death kissed the forehead of a child.
The child brushed away the fly, turned on her side.

The first thought parents have, looking into each
other, passing the infant back and forth, is tears,
is how life hurtles towards a dark climax.
It's natural. Cheese disappears in the ice box.
The sock gets a hole, an opening where death with his
infinity breath is already approaching.
Death tastes vinegar and says, "What lovely wine!"

I'm loaves. I'm fishes now. I wear death
the way others wear jewelry. It glitters at my ears.
It wraps my wrist in silver. It is what stays behind.
It's just death trying to take away my charms. Death
isn't as greedy as I am. He only wants it all
and I'm not willing to give. I pay him off in fragments
of myself, saving the best parts for last.

Last Thoughts

Exactly at the moment of his death
he was imagining melons. Cantaloupe,
honeydew, casaba, watermelon. Neruda's
"Ode to the Watermelon," "fatigue in drops."

Silence. What if he comes to us in melon?
A very funny melon, a ridiculous sitcom
of a melon, three plot lines interwoven
into a final fruity punch.

"Fruit from the thirst tree." What if
the melon is overripe? What if there's
past life but no future, reincarnation
as false as heaven and hell. Maybe just this

life and melon. Maybe not even this life
only melon. When you have a child you bring
more melons into the splashy, laden with flavor
world. Can he read over my shoulder?

Ricardo, where is the last lost melon?
The one that rolled away from your mind
revealing only an empty tomb? Knock back
when I pound a melon for ripeness.

A hollow thunk means, "I'm ready." Dull
thud means, "More time." Three for a "yes."
Two for a "no." Séance of vines. My own
last thought still ripening.

Cracking Myself Up

The watermelon is an aphrodisiac
for the thirst junkies. Desire is
the concession of the troubadours.

Bad news sent good news spinning
and circumstance pounded the kitchen floor.

Antipathy got a handle on apathy.
Rastafarians kept hairdressers
awake all night with dreads.

Manicurists speak sign language
to show off their talent.

The elemental table got drunk at Oh-Kay
Casino, kept losing at roulette.

Even elocutionists get the blues
and mispronounce the names of tides,
ebb and high, spring and neap.

"Get out of yourself," the airplane told the sky.
"I'm all thumbs," the hitchhiker replied.
"So long," the shaggy dog story said to haiku.

Three concubines dressed as men learned to play
their combs. Will there be jug bands in the new
millennium? "I don't know," the washboard hummed.

Loosen up your torsos, Ladies, we are going
through the mail.

What did one literary allusion say
to another? Thoreau?

Sabbath in June 2000

When did prayer fall out of the wine?
Is the moon actually a Necco wafer or TV in 1969?

Can candy eradicate war? How much vodka
did they drink at the summit conferences?

Are sirloin steaks as smart as apples?
Can we forgive cows for feeding us too well?

Do car engines speak Esperanto or Italian?
Is it fair? Is foul, foul?

Is my father's sweat keeping the putting greens alive?
Is golf a sport or an appetizer for martinis?

Is my brother a mensch? Why am I getting so Jewish
now when I have no memory and can't read Hebrew?

Why are moths hyperactive in the sluggish summer evenings?
What substance is the soul of the tree frog who ate a hundred moths?

Is wine happier when the cork is out?
Is Sappho a household word?

Are Laurel and Hardy really friends?
Was Groucho Marx a Marxist?

Is humor married to elegy and if so
who performed the ceremony?

Grieving in Two Languages, Though I Am Monolingual

For Jim Sagel

I'm calling to you, bro, up in Spanglish Heaven
where bilingual angels cruise with custom wings.
Your eyes sure twinkled here, on this crazy planet.
Your voice was a laughter voice, Riverside Drive.

Maybe you cried in two languages. We never saw it,
with a cheerful front, a deck of cards in a dark pocket.
Your stories filled up the dust viejos who told them,
backfilled, like you'd haul in topsoil to a worn-out field.

Your books are still breathing in small bookstores
that don't put much stock in sex and violence.
Children read you, cinnamon toothpicks in their mouths.
A low rider drove through you slowly at night.

Now we all have hydraulic legs, boom box hearts,
airbrushed minds. You were the quietest
conquistador, conquering with sweet affection,
writing the world as flashed in a rearview mirror.

Made me a writer just by the right nudge
toward my own instinct. You gave and gave
then gave up the ghost. Went to that other place,
took refuge in the mystery. Misterioso, no?

Our sadness, the spring frost that takes the apricots.
Now I know why the viejas shake their heads.
I've been shaking mine, swearing out loud,
loca in two languages. I'm left behind

to make lyrics out of truck tire rims. I need you
for advice on the phone, to deconstruct chimichangas,
to discuss the virtues of deep frying and gossip.
You remind me to buy the *Rio Grande Sun*. Española

was your bible. Are you really gone, my dear familiar?
Can I say amigo, me, in my impossible Anglo accent
with honky affiliations? It is no pleasure to write this
without you to laugh in two languages.

Maybe those pachuco angels could climb their ladder
to deliver our prayers of esteem, in case you don't know
how much you were loved. We hold you highly
as you have held us. As you have always been held.

What Caught My Eye*

Would life be richer if the sunflowers blooming
Became tanagers, and feathers flew out of the bird?
Maximillian yellow hit the George Bellows blue sky.

I used to live below the abstract, adobe,
a tract house in the real. Our field flanked
La Mesita, inhabiting John Sloan's Masonite.

Oh Georgia, You drew me, lured by a skull,
a blue feud. I arrived and found a pelvis
by the road, caught is what I know about bone.

I ride this white painted horse home from the *Rendezvous*.
My horse is in oil. My horse is in alfalfa.
A group from India passes between this life and my last.

Two of them take illicit photographs
next to two Hopi dancing in bronze,
a rattlesnake held in teeth.

The man who donated his kidney strolls by.
Life always grabs me, rattle and fear,
though my people rarely handled snakes.

Paint gasps for canvas.
We toss our lives back and forth, smile,
handle what we dare.

* The next four poems were written for the 85th anniversary of the Museum of Fine
Art, Santa Fe, New Mexico. They were performed at the Saint Francis Auditorium,
and then recordings were made available to play alongside the paintings.

Talpa Winter: by Andrew Dasburg

For Thayer Carter

Step back from your life, see how the angles
Intersect. No happy. No sad. Cubism in
The snow. I once Sufi danced in Talpa
Big with child, sang, "Allah, Allah."

We danced eight years after Dasburg painted.
The dust rose. I brought squash pie
And slept there, wood smoke and snow.
The smell of adobe is richer than cubism or Sufism.

Life or art, I've often asked myself.
Choose life, my family says, their forks poised
To eat my day. Choose art, my husband writes
A certificate which I frame.

My heat took the white road home, papered
My life with cool norteño art so I am alive,
Standing here after Freud in Talpa snow.
I know Lombardy poplars with no leaves.

My cooling dreams at night, as white
Born, blue at first, shadowed, crinoline,
Milk on the infant, paint chips, wind chill.
Mornings we woke to gesso white

I needed cubism to give contortions
To my day. By noon we were in mud time.
The morning snow sang *zikhr* before melting.

The Pull North

I have a pulling north. At the Ranchos church
a coffin stood open at the right of the nave. A young man,
beautiful with death, a harsh and stark repose
with no narrative to his body but hush and behold.

Young man with your motorcycle or bullet, cancer
or alcohol, I'll always hold the cold inner church
of your body up to the light as you did not wait
in the most painted church in the state.

We're not built for pleasure, but equal to this sorrow.
Your sad angles hold handprints of mud mixed
with Taoseño tears and straw. You stand and stand.
Man has a tomb and God has a room inside us.

Fritz Scholder

There's a woman in Fritz Scholder, I'm hesitant to say
who has my hair, gray, my glasses,
a long green uniform of paint
and my self-conscious smile. Check her out.

She stands amidst the Arts Faculty at IAIA
at 4:15, 1968 while I was still in a college dorm
getting over my first great love in Massachusetts
knitting gray scarves of northeastern grief.

There I am in paint, waiting for myself
to age into an old New Mexican. Fritz
anticipated me, a crony, tenure track,
collegiality, only along the way I took a turn

tacking my sails on love's winds,
babies and gardens and sidetracks.
A surface of narcissism and philanthropy.
The entire faculty of IAIA lived exemplary

lives without me. They don't remember me,
at the center of their portrait, because I live here
on the other side of canvas, gesturing,
inviting you to time's radiant line dance.

After Horses, Horses

Blanco my horse with arrows aimed down for legs,
with the dull face that in age takes an ascetic cast, my horse
with a starry chin and a chewing heart, with a gourmand's mouth
who could eat for breakfast the Great Plains, with a ladder back,
his back a herd of sheep.

My horse with a dumb back swayed by his twenty years.
My horse with a fetlock of white violins.
With nostrils inhaling fresh bells of air,
with a drink of water in his teeth, with a slurp
as deep and long as Civil War. My horse

with a thirst for song and a water trough of ice.
My horse aging underneath my legs. With as many years
to live as he gets, his *calavera* face underneath my hands.
My horse, a walking skeleton and a running harp.
With an Eohippus in his genes and a Muybridge photograph,

running, running, watch the legs all rise. My horse with a trot
of rocking horse on springs. My horse to escort me to death.
With a ride into my past and a childhood eye. My horse
who moves me back and forth in time, with a canter
I located under my fear. With an easy lope

that's new like my back teeth. With a canter that astounds
and a gallop into owls. My barranca horse, my badlands
steed that the neighbors love to ride, with his yellow teeth,
his teeth of grain, sweet feed, his floated teeth of oats.
My alfalfa-eating horse with an Appaloosa rump

and a quarter horse mind. With an onion-colored rump
and a fish bone stare. With his sweat after running and gentle hoof.
With his hooves under water at Santa Cruz. With his smell
of elk and horse shit perfectly. With his miles.
My horse with his many miles and his canyon floors.

His arroyo mane and his fly switch tail. His sleeping
on his feet and his standing still. My horse as he rolls
after saddle his pig roll, dirt roll, dust storm end of day.
My horse with a backhoe poised to dig his grave.
Apple horse, leather horse, water steed, holding equine court.
My horse who keeps his word, which is none at all.
Honest horse who disdains carrots, gobbles tumbleweed.

I am thankful for my peaceable silver steed. He has no hands
and no money in his thoughts. He has no consternation
about his soul. Puff into his nostrils where he exhales horse.

Blanco Ascending

My horse who changed his name
from Whitey Martínez to Blanco
was last seen eating apples
in a deserted rancho in Chimayó.
We were drinking margaritas
at the Rancho de Chimayó before it burned,
Blanco née Whitey was cruising a small orchard
down the road when he ascended,
making him the world's first holy horse or
maybe they are all divine.

The fence was intact, the neighbors
saw nothing. But next day he was gone.
Apples still bore the imprint of his old teeth,
teeth that always lied about his age
since the day we bought him from
a family in La Villita.

Blanco bore me through sweetness
and betrayals. He suffered everyone
who came to ride, always galloped up
the side of gullies, eternal fat darling of all.

Now he is ascended, garlands of roses.
Some suspect aliens, others say heroin
dealers sold him, turned him into smack.
He didn't escape or would have turned up
at the pasture. No one would steal such
an ancient horse branded on his left flank
with a large angel holding a gun.

So since he vanished standing up in
the village of weavers who weave standing up
he became the keeper of apples, purveyor
of holy dirt, God's mule, white powder
of heroin and cocaine shrouding him forever.

Sacred beast, every day I pray for a sighting,
a miracle on a saddle blanket, a tortilla
burnt like Appaloosa, hoofprints on the clouds.

The Singing Bowl

What we need is more people who specialize in impossible.
—Theodore Roethke

Twenty-Six

Under my daughter who casts so slender a shadow
is the crescent moon, who is the disappearing
woman and the ones disappeared, who laughs
when things get scary, who disappears in beauty,
who cuts through me like knife to room-
temperature butter, who sacrifices herself
for others, who is my heart with too thin legs,
who eats no meat, who has no meat, who is spread
thin, who is my living daughter, who began dying
the moment she took breath, who is my dead father's
granddaughter, who is my living mother's dividend,
who wants to own land, who is exactly half my age,
who doesn't belong to me, who polishes my mirror,
who is my "Am I good enough?" daughter,
who wears a head rag when she cleans house,
who lives in a dungeon like all serving girls,
who will soon rise up, who is busy all the time
not working, who has made her industry motion
and pleasure, who manufactures joy and beauty,
who can't help loving, who is my walking worry,
who sets records for slow blooming, who is not
a forced narcissus or peach branch but absolute
true spring.

Prayer Flags

Not choosing, the girl made choices.
Rosemary will winter-kill at this altitude.

By worry the mother supports not choosing.
Worry is reverse prayer.

If they were Italian, by now they would have chosen,
grape vines, varieties, and locale.

The girl intends either to travel or go to college.
She is either wearing jeans or dressed for salsa dancing.

The apricot tree which bloomed so prettily
is fruited, but the fruits have no flavor

having grown from a pit cast into the garden.
It has a perfect shape.

She has grown so thin. The mother has exclusive rights
on worry. Worry is reverse osmosis.

Reverse osmosis is a way to filter water. The cats value shade
and the honeysuckle pruned to elegance begins to leaf.

The mother knows a parable about cutting a butterfly out of its cocoon.
Prayer flags from the daughter's Nepal trip hang on the porch.

Sun and wind released the prayers, faded
into air they may have saved a marriage.

Calmly the girl gives the mother advice to study yoga.
In May a flowering locust goes magenta.

The father says it skips a generation
but does not specify what "it" is.

Last week's wind storm littered the portal
with fine dust in swirls and wads of leaves.

The two women are experts in divergent realms
and oppose each other like thumb and forefinger.

One Note

I'm about to give birth, no,
It is my daughter carrying.
I have just died, no, not me,
It was my mother waving I love you
To my niece. I am a little angry at my family.
They let my mother die. They are a little angry
At me, I let my daughter become pregnant
In the light of a rainbow at Santa Clara Canyon.

Where, on pine needles, is this mother hiding?
Where, on the side of a mesa, is a baby
Hanging upside down considering
What being human means? Meanwhile,
I hum and play a singing bowl. My instrument
Because it only has one note like I do.

Each of us goes on singing the small tunes
We learned from place and person, city
Of Pittsburgh and village, La Puebla,
The beauty shop, the stores. Automobiles
Know us better than our family does. Our shoes
Wear out their lives carrying us around.

The Singing Bowl

I.

A bronze singing bowl my daughter
Brought me from Nepal. Diameter
Of a woman dilated to deliver.
I was thinking about pushing today,
I never told her how childbirth felt.

At 6:00 a.m. I read about Chinese prostitutes,
Children stolen, bound feet, dead by twenty.
Twenty was old then at Gold Mountain City.
By nine I had cried. By ten who knows
What realization will occur? Have faith

The birds would be the first to tell me
If they had need for words. Light on the bowl.
Light in my daughter's scarred heart.
She carries beauty like a courtesan.
I sat at Eldorado coffee shop, admired her

Apron tied under the head of my grandchild.
Meant for beauty and to serve love. Why not?
Women do not run the world, and yet
I'm ready for the wars to end. Circles
Of dissidents and prophets. "Use your words,"

A mother tells a tantrum child. "Go to your room!"
An old woman says to Arafat, Sharon.
This baby coming, a clangor for a singing bowl.
My daughter with her pierced nose,
Her belly gone awry with love.

II.

She got me a singing bowl and a bracelet that said,
OM MANE PADME HUM. But was it before or after
the accident Thanksgiving Day? I'm thinking before,
since after she was in shock and had to split Nepal
so I don't think she was in a shopping frame of mind
this young woman who loved shopping and loved me
and was able to love on a planetary scale because
they were just coming back from a trek and riding
on top of the bus, there was no room inside, when
something invisible, for it was dusk and you know how
dusk messes with the eyes especially in Nepal with Buddha
eyes on everything, so nobody could see or can figure out
what hand of fate came and struck her friend in the face
splitting it and breaking her arm, her leg, five teeth, a hand
of God, a branch, a wire. She fell onto my daughter, maybe
six inches lower, sitting right on the roof and not her backpack,
and they kept her out of shock and got her to Pokara
where the hospital was rank and the doctor reluctant.
She lived, though her right arm is useless.
She's a photographer. The flight home cost more than my house.
The police wanted to hang the bus driver. The girls
wouldn't give his name. Corina came back early
though already too late, pierced her nose in LA
while visiting her friend in the hospital. Brought
me gifts, a bowl that holds singing and begging
and thanking, somebody else's daughter,
hammered by hand, by an unknown hand
in Katmandu, Nepal or maybe Pokara.

III.

Gazing down at herself, becoming unbecoming
While cells multiply, brain, testicles or more.
Inside her fertile Wonder Womb
Navel to nascent navel calling, she alters.

Wild cells organize, brain, spinal cord, ovaries or more.
From lightning rod sex and mountain air, double rainbow.
Navel to nascent navel calling, she's an altar.
In the clearing a girl her mother won't let go woman.

From the lightning rod of sex and Santa Barbara air.
The final countdown, everybody shifts, the family hedges.
In the clearing a girl her mother can't let go woman,
tight as they are, another being comes between.

The final countdown, everybody edgy, the family shifts
We do and do not mind. Her lover paints.
Tight as they are, another being comes before the wedding.
She qualifies for Medicaid. He paints million dollar houses.

We do and do not mind. Her lover paints
This vast beauty, head down to face its maker.
She qualifies for Medicaid. He paints on canvas.
She serves coffee for eight bucks an hour including tips.

This vast beauty, head down to face its maker.
Who made this child, man and ground, woman and rain?
She serves coffee for eight bucks an hour.
A Muslim woman prays in Arabic for easy passage.

Who made this child, double rainbow?
Holding her belly, uncovered at the market
a Muslim woman prays in Arabic for easy passage
kisses her belly with her permission.

Holding her belly, revealed and marked,
inside this Wonder Womb, fertile
kisses. Her belly grows with her permission.
She gazes at herself becoming.

Singing Down

I'm coming. Down out of the clouds
into the rain. I hope I'm coming straight
and clear. I hope I'm falling on holy ground,
That the people catching me are sure and loving.

I hope the people bringing me to earth
have said their evening prayers and their morning prayers,
because where I'm coming from is made of prayers and leaves.
Silk spun from mulberry is fine but where I'm coming from is
finer still.

You know those shape singers with notes so bright
they drop, note by note, into your body?
That's how I'm singing down into a woman
dressed in gauzy skirts next to a man whistling

to hold up. I'm the one calling down the lullabies.
I'm yours. I am your DNA gone wild with love,
I am the split second the angels take to connect us
to God, my spine the ladder up and back.

My feet haven't yet touched down
so learn the old songs for me
because I'll come out dazed and start forgetting.
My eyes will gaze at you and I'll lose

my angel sense. Sing me to ease
with an anthem from my dazzling alma mater.

Birth Song*

Male without enemy
I am the lover's exhaling.
In the pain light, the cold light
the five-fingered one.

Under the hand I am the center
of stroking, my warm parts, my live skin,
mystery in the dim house
with a birth smell of whelp.

My cord cut,
Small Ten Toes, I am the tern's wing,
my father's foot, walrus tusk.

Wrap me in flannel, I am the sunrise
all summer. I am the seal man, flat
otter tail, the sunset all winter.

I am the caught one, the fish line,
your first son. I live with the inhale
and talk your soft tongue.

I am the cheek on the nipple,
the sounds under ice floes. Whale milk,
I am the peacekeeper, day breaker.

Sew me a skin pouch.
Hide all your money there, your north wind,
your dark moon, the song mothers sing.

* This poem was inspired by a series of Inuit songs translated by Muriel Rukeyser
and Paul Radin from texts collected by Knud Rasmussen.

Labor

The eyes of the horse in pain are too deep to fall into.
The sight of a baby's head between her legs.
The tree is called Betchel's Crab, flowers like crinoline.

My husband quits his job and cannot settle at night.
When I drive over the pass towards Glorieta
my heart becomes a Baptist.

I want to answer the phone and say "Holy Family."
At Chimayó I filled my purse with holy dirt
as a Saturday prayer for childbirth.

On Sunday I was putting nickels on Ganesh,
remover of obstacles. The young man is so strong
and loves her ridiculously. On Monday, the baby.

The pansies and dianthus he planted are vigorous
like Telluride, Aspen, Taos, anyplace mountainous.
He is leaning into his car while my daughter naps.

I ask people, "Do I look changed?" and they don't answer.
The head of the baby against my chest,
as if happiness burst out of my mother's old heart.

I talk out loud to my mother in her car I inherited.
Tears make driving Impressionist. I pull over,
Monet. I weep, Vincent Van Gogh. I rejoice, Degas.

A beautiful dancer is killed on Rodeo Road.
The dust off our pasture dances
as we are in drought.

On Mother's Day the brown horse has to be put down.
The new father tells me, "Life is so transient."
My daughter's breasts in the mirror so full of milk.

West of Eden

Our first act was planting, in exile from green.
Before we had water we hauled water.
We planted two of everything. Half died.
We planted Hope's placenta under cottonwood.

You should be forty to study Kabala.
There is a Tree of Life with a right and left,
a kind, compassionate, female side, the right
brain of the Tree of Life and a left brain side.

When my grandson was born I was present.
In forty-five minutes the placenta hadn't come.
The midwives said, "If not now, when?"
Within minutes the afterbirth, a second motion.

They marveled how healthy it was, turned
it over and the white umbilical branched
into a perfect Tree of Life. They pointed this
out and named it. Holy holy holy.

His father's hand and his mother's heart.
His father's heart and his mother's hand.
From Adam, the earth, comes Galen.
From Eve, who made it happen, comes Galen.

And it is up to us to match Eden which heavens us,
balance blessings, draw the spiritual waters down
where we smell fresh. Advice from the tree of life,
our first text as we are cut from God.

Glorieta Baby Poem

My baby who is not my baby
You create frescoes on my body, I think of you, akimbo,
and smell curry and melon cooled by your vowels.

You flourish and I demure. Secure
in your mother's embrace with your
Ashkenazi gene pool and Alabama smile.

Your face, little doctor, mends my shish kebab heart.
You perform an appendectomy on my assumptions
and I fall into the shameless iambic pentameter of love.

I love you like Federico García Lorca loved
Cuba and Castile, like William Butler Yeats loved
Ireland his Ireland, like the Brontës loved the moors.

My charisma is quieted by your glowing amber.
I live on the edge of enamel, your four small teeth.
I hope we never clash. I promise you new shoelaces.

You are the dividend, I am the crashing stock.
You are the flowering locust, I am the saltbush,
so many tributaries converge in your amazed pond.

Someday the flumes of testosterone will croon into you,
but for now this river will carry. The 2:00 p.m. train whistles
past, we call it the Nap Train. My silver heart in your close hand.

Our Baby So Smart

He's going forward like a windup toy
On tracks of milk. He's got an IQ
Of water splash, a heart of sound waves.

His tracks are the tracks the stinkbug
Leaves in dust. His halo follows him
Late like an afterthought of clean wash.
Like the Virgin Mary snapped her fingers.

He leaves a wake of rose scent and tidal
Love. The ocean grows forgetful when he
Waves good-bye. When he makes the
Motion of water, the drought ends.

Gentle rain in his face. Too soon,
Will and the ego of camels, the ego
Of cats, the ego of elk will well up.
But for now a one-year vine

Flaunts clematis flowers the size
Of his head. He sniffs geranium
And covers his non-ascetic face
In ashes. He makes pleasure a sacrament.

He naturalizes the landscape with vowels.
He says, "Hot hot hot" and points, to table,
To locust tree in pink flagrant bloom.
The world is all hot to his cool cruise.

He backs down an entire flight of stairs
Like an air traffic controller, self-possessed,
Jaunty, you expect him to doff his cap
But he can't fathom the word "doff."

His cap is "Hot hot hot." When motion
Stops he is a mandolin of sleep. His eyes
Arrest the birds and send them to jail.
His dreams speak Belgian and Hungarian.

His nightmares have no claws.
The whole world is breast and light.
He knows no other name for it.

Genealogy

He asked me where he was when his mother was my baby.
I said, you were in mystery. I didn't know,
couldn't say heaven. I could say
you were your face before you were born.

Later, I was praying the last gasp of night prayer
so he would finally settle down, after the three books,
after the Three Bears and the Three Little Pigs,
after the boy, age three, held me like a spinning top

to see how long before I'd topple. After he hid in a hut
of straw bales, in that finale of prayer I said all sorts of things
to God, out loud, as if I were a child alone, not aged
with this new child in my bed.

He's from accident, the urge to life, unplanned.
From a mother born out of Sufi dancing and peyote
tea, a father from Birmingham, two uncertainties who met
on the street of a ghost town and danced a little.

He came into body, danced out. The beauty of his crowning.
Every child, the old Jews say, could be Messiah.
He came from clear back to Russia and Hungary
and my husband's Belgian work ethic, the pinpoint

at the end of genealogy. He's from chance encounter. Rainbows
should be mentioned here. Beer and marijuana.
But all I could say was you were in mystery. Nobody
I know really knows. If they do they're not telling.

I'm the great mother who gets tired. You're the new engine,
America. I feel the way grandmothers feel
in times of war, tears under the skin, liquidity,
and you're absorbing, without trying, all of me.

Slamming Back Milk

From the center of my days comes milk
As if I were a breast not a car driver
Not an e-mail addict, not a surly shopper
Or a credit card swiper, not and certainly
Not a cow or a goat or a camel.

This is the milk you might call lace,
The last vapor of the jet contrail, a swimmer turning
A lap, a fascination with quilts, a quarter spinner,
An enthusiasm for Shar-Peis, a glint of light
Off of a baritone, a steam room filled with Jews,
A manacle, a harmonium.

It could be Allen Ginsberg's milk
Or cement mixer unloading its river of aggregates
Or the river itself, my God, the Rio Grande or
An inoculation against flu, what I mean is Life Force.
Life Force. Hear what I have to say? Opal pulchritude,
Oh studious one, Scholar of Kabala.

Mystic, at the center of my chest is a rehearsal dinner
For the bilingual wedding. Mariachi band,
Viennese waltz, a little tango and basketballs,
The girls jumping rope and missing. Milk,
The last supper. Milk, the missing teen. Milk,
The shed kimonos. Milk the aficionados of olives.

Liquidity and milk. Got milk? The moustache of
Literal bovine mammary secretions because I survived
Two winters in Wisconsin on the dairy farm
And have heifers forever before me, staring at me,
Cutting through me in honest cow meditation.

At the center of my days, creamy and fluid,
Malleable and filling all crevices, bottles of life
Force, the froth of it, steamed for cappuccino,
The latte of late, the cow of now. This hot milk
Flows. Milk of human kindness. Mother of cloud.
Mother of teeth. The anti-war. The urge to lactate Peace.

Morning Poem

Hearing my grandson's voice is the all-clear sound
At the end of the air raid.
And my daughter's voice isn't as much lament
As pale tissue paper, voile, camellia or peony.

And the love of my life is a wanderer who landed
In my braids, building a timber frame house there.
Got lost in my hair for a hundred days when he meant
To spend one night, dreaming of north woods

And other women, and why shouldn't he?
And the holy man singing isn't as much a mystic
As a rock star battling forest fires with a guitar.
And Los Alamos isn't a town from 1953 frozen

In Cold War aspic but a community of millionaires
Funded by government and God to keep the bombs
Cooked and ready to serve at the banquet called
Armageddon. Just saying that word is a badly designed

Prayer. And the rabbits are not tiny destroyers,
Grasshoppers disguised as rodents, but childhood,
Beatrix Potter and even pests can give pleasure
On a morning like this.

And my own body isn't so much a sacred vessel
Of breath, pleasure and pain running rivers,
As it is an elephant of love. Enough now, enough then,
Enough history and even enough suddenly
Becomes full. Who could have filled enough
In the night while I was sleeping?

Three Poems for Mundo

1. I want to say the word *Mundo* as this week
I met baby Mundo, a Dutch kid, barely toddling,
saying the baby words for cat and fish, a serious baby.

Saying, "Buddha, Buddha." My own grandchild smiles
all the time, with her two cut teeth and her flock of hairs.
Almost too happy, I hug her to get the happy

to rub off. She infects me with joyful futuristic music.
She piles my regrets with blocks and knocks them down.
All week under the snow I was alive.

The elder staving off death, seven phone calls,
a roll of tape. Postage. The eye of the needle
I pass through is never roomy enough.

No company here and yet I am a sociable person
when I'm not busy perfecting my pessimism,
I broke a mirror. I accepted a red gift.

I made a baby named Mundo a love song
on a blackboard. I turned him into
the love of my life this week.

Mundo, Mundo, can your hip Dutch parents coax
a better world for your footsteps? I lived some other way
this week. Became Hopi. More survival, more prayerful.

I miss God and yesterday in the wingspan of the raven
I felt a little sacred breath. In the rescued bobcat
with my name, in the book on the shelf that held you,

in spiritus sanctus of imagined cathedrals,
in the cave of the owl, in the snow, in the snow, in
the snow. I met a child called Mundo. My own daughter

named Hope is on the phone. The burning world keeps me warm.
In the snow. I love this chilling, sequined world.
Mundo.

2. Mundo, dear baby, dear reader
who can't even read.
Things are getting pretty dicey so it's good
that you have a Buddha in your house to tell you
mellow out, when the going gets rough.
You are the Uber-Toddler. You are the child
Saint Nicholas had in mind when he invented gifts.

I didn't tell you, my youngest has fallen in love.
It only just happened. I wish you could see them.
They give off a glow like your pure light.
They are toddling their new love through town
where people feel blessed by them. Angels come
to mind and also all the old love stories.

Sometimes love turns out. You are an example.
Love comes with a big warning sign. Twice marriage
had global warming like a curse. Love lasted.
Will last, is always born and hovering.
I named my youngest Hope, and she walks
through the world giving off sparks, like you.

Baby Mundo, giving me faith in the year
that could be rough. I don't know, I sense
chaos around every corner. It could be me
when I get too happy, The Evil Eye my old Jews
would say. Mundo, we can't even praise a baby.
My ancestors would spit to ward off bad tidings.

Good tidings to you and all of your Dutch kin.
I met a child named Mundo and I wish Hope
could meet you. But you are gracing
the Netherlands, a low-lying place.
You will always have a place in my heart.

I send you oceans of love, little Mundo.
This year or the next I will see you grown,
until then, diminutive visionary, I send you peace.

3. What He brings into the house
On Chanukah it was a red-tailed hawk
Gasping, we could looks down its esophagus
As he held it in leather gloves, its smashed hip
Crippling it as the lit candles still burned.

Or the time he brought the bull snake
Wrapped around his neck into the bathroom
While I lazed in the tub. After a jolt of shock
The boys-will-be-boys smirk rises on my face

Or the moonlight he placed in the windows,
Or the chickens he's always bringing in for some
Odd reason. The bins of red worms he moved in
As weather got rough. Or the women

How they showered in our greenhouse shower,
Their body rinsed where mine had stood
Their bodies gone places mine had gone.
One in torn clothing and one in a velvet cape.

Or the thorns he attached to lilac.
Or the roses he escaped from. Concentration
Camps of love, and then he brought fresh wind.
The doors are always open when I come home.

He opens, I close. He aerates. I conserve.
We both bring here our manners, soft and hard.
I have to tell you, Mundo, Your parents will do no better.
Your future lovers could do worse.

So Far From Pittsburgh

⪘

Mabel Dodge Luhan wrote to a friend back east,
"I have no news. Nothing happens here but miracles."

Pittsburgh Encore

In the McGee Hospital for women
with its revolving nurses.
Under anesthesia on a Saturday

before my father's golf foursome,
I incarnated, a kvetch and an ingrate.
In August, between Leo and Virgo

I was showered with blessings,
a refrigerator, Howdy Doody, central air.
I chose the curses, heir of the war

felt entitled to my little mantle of pain.
Sharp and shapeless was my mother's love.
Bountiful was my father's wallet.

I took lessons in everything, piano, tap.
I was a child. My only art was whining
though I learned how to be bourgeois

and hide in the closet with Mark Twain.
Mark Twain was a bourgeois with an accent.
My accent was steel and slag.

I had Gerald Stern's teeth and Jack Gilbert's
chest only they lived in Paris, visiting whores.
Harry Rubin stomped in the upper apartment.

We moved away from the noisy Jews
into a mixed neighborhood
with English street names.

All the houses had labels on the doors
that said, we're trying hard.
My mother was beyond me

but tried to drag me along
scuffing my patent leather good girl
Mary Jane's on the holocaust.

My father whistled in the door.
I dreamed of Peter Pan and gave to UNICEF.
It was a new world.

Amana. Westinghouse. Praise God.
Pass the Worcestershire sauce.
There was love so dark, I wouldn't even taste it.

Ellsworth Avenue

My mother sang, "You Are My Sunshine."
I lived in the basement of a brick house,

dreamed Peter Pan had leprosy, wolves lived
in the laundry chute among my father's underwear and socks.

It was after the war I was born. Our music teacher taught
"Happy Days Are Here Again" on the melody flute.

My dog, Mr. Chips, chased his tail. I put my hand
into his whirling circle of cur, already keen for the bite.

I lived alone. I ate books, kept my hands
off my genitals. I crouched at the top of my closet

when I was angry, reading *A Connecticut Yankee
in King Arthur's Court*, the first chapter over and over.

Now my house is sold to a doctor.
His wife is a doctor too, they have children.

He was mowing his lawn. He invited me in.
I asked, "Is the green barn out back still standing?"

It was a place horseless carriages sat, oil
dripped, and I climbed to an attic of newsprint

left from the thirties. he said, "No."
I said, "No."

I kept my house intact.
There are invitations I never accept.

Imagine How Salty

money tastes after it's been handled by countless fingers.
That's how my father tasted after golf.
He fed me pistachios, Shah of Iran brand,
over his martinis and my ginger ale.
He rinsed the chill off of the ice.
This shell in my hand the color of bars he frequented
with his friend Ubby. The gin-wet surface shined.

He wanted me to be comfortable. I lived in slums,
carried all my own water for seven years. Heated
with wood. He adjusted central air conditioning.
Who controls the dials? He wanted
me but he wanted his pleasure more.
Thumbelina dance, Thumbelina sing.
I performed puppet shows and Harry Belafonte.
He was Harry too. I learned Hebrew
so I could mourn with him.

After I die it will be smooth and dark
and cradled. The great rocking and the greater
soothing I am so afraid of despite all my books.
Then I will be shell, and into Maternal again.
Poetry is one fourth of death, its bliss and pull
and terror. When this shell splits open.
When eternity cracked, I came out.
My father gave rise to my birth so I could memorize him.

Aleph Bet Gimmel I forget, but I know my lost father.
The shells, the shells, shtetl and pogrom.
The afterlife comes next, riding this horse out
on a nutshell saddle. The lie the rabbi told me
I refute, that we live on in memory only.
We live on in car brakes and window glass,
five o'clock shadows and dinner platters.
We live on in the empty syllable of G-d's name,
endless breath between "G" and "D."

The Angels of Pittsburgh

The angels of Pittsburgh have no bells in their names.
Pittsburghers swallow final vowels, a strange repast
eaten in immigrant languages. Angels become angls,
losing the very syllable seraphim long to inhabit.

Russian and Polish angels with hands in pockets slouch,
forget to sing. Working class angels with drab caps,
jackets full of rebar, steel toed boots. They smoke.
They love their family, hang out in corner bars.

These are the saddest angels in America, with unspellable
eastern European names and Old Country food nobody
makes right anymore. They fought in the war, sit on
skeletal skyscrapers. Pittsburgh is their Paris, their Berlin.

Andrew Carnegie endowed Pittsburgh. He wanted to grow wings.
Impress God. His heaven is an old library next to a museum
with reconstructed dinosaur bones. He rides ghost streetcars
down Ellsworth, veers left at Neville past a vacant garage.

Takes Fifth Avenue all the way downtown. The conductor,
a sore throat lozenge in his mouth, shouts out stops.
Museums. Pitt. Children's Hospital. Mercy. The Hill.
Carnegie pulls the wire to ring the bell, leaving the trolley

filled with angels. I've ridden next to sad angels, sodden
wings hidden in suit coats. I was born there, love grief,
a native of gravity. My mother flew off to groom and bleach.
My father fixed the knot of his necktie in a mirror

inhabited by angels. Whenever I sing, my back
is to East Liberty, my front to the Monongahela.
Three rivers pour out of me, unceasingly, and the Angel
of Learning who lives in Oakland is my voice coach.

I ride the barges with angels, up through the locks,
and they inform me God moved back to Pittsburgh
to kick back with steelworkers who pray him here.
Unemployed until eternity, they need him closer.

Sacrifice

For Gerald Stern

I am interested in the thin high river,
not the diamond cutter with his eye to the gem.
Don't talk to me after Kol Nidre,
tell me the women's clothing is too loud.

I want to shout over the waterfall,
not table talk, a good woman would say.
But she's not here to squelch me.
She left, first one breast, then the other,
the whole nude chariot ascended.

What am I willing to sacrifice? My hair,
my mother, my house and familia? My brother
grown tall in the hall of the banker?
What damage I inflict is done in the name of love,
as I'd cross myself passing a Catholic Church
because my hands know no other way to say God.

I am not a Jew. Who am I kidding?
At my father's funeral the rabbi spoke,
"Would you sleep on the floor and study Torah?"
I'll sleep on a king-sized bed, next to the same
form of God for three decades. What I'll study
will be the night and the voices, that generous
text and the morning.

I'm not asking the doctor the prognosis.
I'm telling you the name of the virus.
Diamonds burn at extreme heat.
Must I heat my good house with diamonds?

In France they wear a river of diamonds.
It's the role of the cutter to free them.
So many ways to make holy, a desert, a mitzvah,
a leaning. Crack me open you'll find a thin river
and an old Jewish man with an eyepiece,
hunched over, chipping at diamonds.

That Other City

I come from that city. I am now living
in the city of lost beauty, but I may
return to that first city. I am now living
on three acres of heaven and three acres
of hell. I am now counting the chickens,
the cacti; three Araucanas, limitless prickly pear.

I am now watching my neighbors age as we wave
across arroyos and gullies, alcohol and hearts,
betrayal and flash flood. I am now moving into
another heart with less acreage. My mother
is gone. My father is gone. My old marriage
is shaking its finger at me.

In the city where the women are always
beautiful, I am thinking about reading
about Now. A bestseller. In the old
days people didn't need to read about it.
They helped themselves. I am sitting with my heart
as a concave bowl for your convexity.

I am now living with your charity
spooned against my heart and with this
configuration there is space beyond
monogamy. Love in a new context. I am next.
I am now next and then previous.
I am next of all. I am new to next, not sure

if it is a place or another body, a situation.
I am now not sure, but next is possible
as then was. I may return to the other city
or I may linger here. There the women
are my daughter's age. I came from there.
An old man said, "Where you are now

I was once and where I am, you will become."
He said, "It is better to take things off
than to have nothing to put on." I am now
stealing lines from a man named Napo,
father of Leopoldo. I heard them last week
but this is now, in the new city.

Autobiography of Success and Failure

I was born at a women's hospital, in the city called *Success and
Failure*. My mother forgot the doctor's name, she was sleeping at
the time. She returned to work after five days and I was raised up
by women who came from the streets of difficulty to live in our
  house.
At fifteen my hair flipped up, I wore glasses; my nose was my
  father's.

I asked the teacher. I asked the college professors, but success
and failure got all the good grades. When I walked down street
I could be wearing a jacket of success or a cape of failure.
I had two children in the Seventies, one in the Eighties.
I had my children at home giving birth to flowers.

I gave birth to crying and feeding. I brought out of my body
a hundred jobs and a thousand pleasures. I brought out of my belly
three children named Yes, Yes, and Yes. I married at twenty-three,
  cried
for the loss of my life. When my father died I was half gone myself
but I came back the following year, started singing.

If I had to rank love and art I would call them one body.
I predicted my death. It will be in August, a day crossed
by a lizard. I didn't write for seven years, I grew lettuce,
sewed cowboy shirts. My husband and I love to fight
more than spend money. Success and failure

had their heyday in the Fifties. We live in a house we built
totally heated by success and air-conditioned by failure.
If we had a swimming pool we'd skim it with a net to scoop
off the failure. "La vie en rose" is my favorite song.
When I kiss you both plus and minus signs are left on your cheek.

Famous Kisses

. . . fare well perfect mammal.
Fare thee well, from thy silken couch and dark day!
—Michael McClure, *Ghost Tantras* 39

If I had to choose between kissing Marilyn Monroe
or Einstein I would be stumped. I'd pick Marilyn of course
for her lips had the attention of America, had that much charge
and Joe DiMaggio's home run in them, Arthur Miller's last
line, and they kissed Clark Gable and felt his moustache.
I know that Marilyn tasted of purple conversation hearts,
those packets of candy with slang you buy for Valentine's
and the purple, like her lipstick, a little bitter.
Einstein is meanwhile tapping me on the shoulder, whispering
"Space is love" in my left ear. But Marilyn has me now
with her one shoe dangling from her toe and the eternal
subway grate blowing up under her dress and her legs also
part of the way she kisses. I'm melting at Marilyn's moist
overture, her apertures like Nikon cameras in dim light,
wide open. Kissing Marilyn is American as a California
morning. It's reels of film in silver cans that only live
for screens. Light breaks out. Peace breaks out. Death
breaks me open and I'm kissing Marilyn Monroe to learn to be
the best kisser in America. Then Einstein gets my attention.
He tickles me with his white erotic hair, hair
with the energy of atom, of microwave. I can feel
him through my clothes. And for one minute I turn from
the perfect mammal to the man of mind over matter. I lean
over to him. He kisses me on the cheek. I become younger.
I love backwards. My heart is a ten-year-old's and I'm traveling
through space into a perfect equation of love.

How I Got Here

With thanks to Lisa Gill

I got here by daughter and by rain.
If I weren't a mother would I be a train
or a clarinet. Today's rain while I talk
to you on the phone about your lover
and his teacher, soothes me. That rain
because I can get all knotted up in happiness.

Gentle Rain is my maiden name I don't use
except as mantra. I don't have a sign
over my beauty salon that says GENTLE RAIN.
My mother hung out a shingle and cut hair,
colored it blond, platinum or ash, honey by
Revlon and Clairol, I knew them all.
Their stories joining the immortals.

I used to be old and then I loved children.
I used to be gentle rain and then I lived
with flash flood. I never lived in north woods
or a trailer, but I've lived in Chicago and the like,
San Francisco three years after The Summer
of Love. I got here by cities and by dairy farm.
I lived among cows twenty months, their stare and cud,
they were my closest neighbors.

I got here by a peace sign on a woman's black coat
that led me to you and to this place,
this right now, among the other losses
and gunshots, the scar on my belly
and the one on my knee. I got here.
That was plenty. Dear Right Now,
I want to say, Dear Could Have Been
Otherwise. How the tributaries of any life

lead us to each other, this intersection.
I got here by subway and streetcar,
by atomic bomb, Los Alamos led me here
and Santa Clara Pueblo, the dancers danced
me, I rode here on an old horse named Blanco.
I was white. I fell fast in love.
I didn't love desert. I always loved people first
and the landscape came dragging its heels.

How to Get to My House

Graduate from college, then turn left at Pittsburgh
In 1969 and drive through pelting rain
Into Chicago. Fall in and out of love twice then
Take a Blue Volkswagen west. Follow the sunset
With wagon trains in your trunk, decide between
Las Vegas and the desert, go to the end of the earth
And smell Pacific. Watch the sunset 365 times in San
Francisco, get married once, then head northeast
For three days to the place where cows stare
You down and calves suck your fingers. Live there
Two winters. Be brave in the sub-zero heartland.
Clean barns, then head out in a Red Chevy truck with two cats
And a husband and all your best clothing, aim
South and camp in a teepee, mosey west through
Tennessee and Texas. Land in April in Pojoaque
Where there is no water in the rivers, where
Ravens think they own everything, where
Black Mesa stood tall over San Ildefonso dancers
At Easter. Become a settler. Stay put. Buy six acres
And pour all your love and money into it for thirty years.
Here I am, turn right at the arroyo, snake onto Placitas
Past the Gun Club, then first left, and at our house
you are always turning right, right? Go past where there is no
white horse. I am waiting for you to find me.
I am not young, not lost, a homesteader in the steady.
You have navigated well. You have arrived at peace.

On the Beatific Rag

I feel like the wife of a beatnik poet, folding hip platitudes
of wash, defrosting huge chunks of eternity, cooking for the masses,
slinging holy hash. My house smells like New York or the Bay,
full of cats and mattresses. My life's a cookout when you never
know how many will show up, canned beans, whiskey, a sunset
with a gong. Like the longhaired beat wife of a longhaired poet,
shooing children in nightgowns to a far-out place on a down planet.
Sitting around a wobbly table, hacking at a piece of tough meat
called Every Day. I am no-nonsense making lemonade and cleaning
the refrigerator on the longest most beautiful necklace of days
called summer in New Mexico. If you visit I won't clean up
for you, yet summer is one large party with me the caterer.

The problem here is, I am the poet, my own wife, the poetry
chick of this nuclear nuclear family. Just like the wife of Neal
Cassady or the lovers of Kerouac, or going on fire lookout,
following Gary Snyder up some scree.

I feel like Diane Di Prima's worst dream, trying to clean an
    uncleanable scenario. Carrying cleanser and a bottle of vodka,
    my boredom
appearing on TV talk shows and the host says, "And now we have a
guest from that fabulous far flung era, The Beat Generation!"
    I enter
with a feather duster. I'm holding my slim volumes. Jazz plays while
    I read, snapping my
fingers, about lost love like the last gasp, weirded out wife of myself,
    an unknown beatnik poet.
One who loved
to drive carpools, as if New Mexico were just created for her own
mundanity.

Great Little Cars

For Larry

The man who sold me my used car
is leaving. He is going to live in Texas
and take care of horses worth more than I am.

That he knew my brother in the old days
of back east, or that he ended up owning
my mother's car are mere oddities

in his life. In mine, they make for a line
or two in a poem, a story I tell and never
spend enough time reading

like a dream to decipher what it means.
In mid-dream there is a Nambé Pueblo man
and Vietnam. How can I show enough respect?

On my business card I put *"Married a long
long time."* That way I live in a cake safe,
a chocolate keeper with a lock.

And the man who sold me my car
has his own fish to fry. So I meet him for lunch
driven in a classic white Chevy pickup

to say *Adieu* which means *to God, Adios,*
which means *to God* also. *Au revoir*
means we'll meet again which isn't

exactly the point. *Salaam.* Our lives
are embedded in the flesh and net
of the universe. Farewell is what I mean,

waving my dead mother's ironed hankie.
Love always comes driving a used car.
My definitions have nothing to do with it.

Change

The thing is, I am here again and the thing is
I am starting out happy and will have to work toward sadness
and the thing is I used to be sadness's handmaiden, its vestal virgin,
and the thing is I know deep sadness will come again, is in the cards
will shower me in flood or Gentle Rain.

The thing is I am this lifetime of olives
and the thing is always the adequate symbol, Ezra Pound said
and he loved images but hated Jews, and the thing is he was crazy
and eventually was locked up but the thing is

his poems were unlocked and still have a life. *Cantos, Cantos
Cantos*, a book so thick it should have three names.
And the thing is I haven't read him since college but could never sell
his book and the real thing is nobody in my family would ever read
Cantos and so at my death maybe I should be burned with Ezra
Pound and maybe then he would love Jews and realize we had a
certain job to do on earth much as he did and the thing is he loved
Hilda Doolittle and I never met her but her poems are signed H.D.

I'm glad I am alive even if they are not, see how the sadness crept in,
with me it does. The thing is it is my job to yin the yang, to balance
the world of 10,000 sorrows with the 10,000 joys and you know the
thing is at Bode's Store when she rang up my pretzels, chocolate,
and X-ACTO knife and I gave her a ten and two pennies and the
register promised $10,000 in change and the thing was she didn't
have that much so she gave me a smile.

Winter Air

The air was friendly as cellophane.
Three children carved a pumpkin out
of the house. Lit its windows with their lives.

My dead dogs who had split the scene
were barking when I drove up. A small Swiss
Maiden with little innocence borrowed
the VCR, returned it. Her lipstick of pomegranate
keeps me from returning from the underworld.
I slap my husband a mystical high five.

He recycles my existential kisses. We go on living
in the village of La Puebla without blame,
walk the hill to the solar fire station.
The owls were carrying my cat away. His large
palomino body lifted by talons. Fare well Galaxy
son of Mo Mo. Fare thee well Swiss Miss.

We drink from a well we dug inside our bodies.
Egyptians call relationship *Invisible Painting*.
He and I are incognito Rembrandts. We eat Van Gogh
dinners sipping our Matisse wine. A loquacious chicken.
A piddle of salad and a roll. The rain
falls like love in the village of La Puebla.

It comes in absence or torrent as love does.
Saint Ideology, the righteous being, must have been right
and has blessed us. We plant a catalpa next to a yucca

next to the vinca beside the ginkgo. On Paradise
we feast. There are no enemies in the wild, each tree
is perfect. The one called enemy becomes my teacher.

We kiss the knuckles of invading armies.
They taste vaguely of pomegranate.
The seasons arrange themselves like slot machines.
We go on living till we die in La Puebla
without preferences like the Third Chinese Zen Patriarch.
This life, white orbs of aster after frost.

Consolation

The asters are ecstatic, all night during the thieveries
and robbers, the asters against the sky. Early autumn
the asters are flagellates, the asters are penitents.
I am about to fast. I am asking for absolution. The asters
ask nothing, ask me to violate no trust.

I say, "I will not lie. Will not steal."
Wastrel, they accuse, the asters are astute.
They hammer knowledge of beauty into the air.
They study war no more, gain ground by roots in beauty.
The asters ask me could I not parlay

their beauty into money. I could not and told them.
I refer them to my doctor. I say, morning glory,
yarrow, I tell myself, mullein. It stays understated
but the asters are ecstatic. They sing without their clothes on.
They are Symphyotrichum in chorus. Voices a capella

like Caravaggio coming out of darkness, lit from above.
Voices like king's velvet, no small consolation.
They tutor me in beauty and finales, the fine fettle asters.
I graduate Summa cum asters. Magna cum sunflowers.
The asters are my inquisition. Tell me about where you live,

about its particular despair. I answer hypodermic, robbery.
The asters are saint and salvage. They sing Gregorian Chant
down a long muddy road. A form of godhead, the nasty
and the sacred when roots go down to draw up purple
out of dust, rain down God in purple rays.

Treeing

Is the verb of the noun.
An attempt to enter the being state of trees,
stand beside a tree for thirty years,
but I don't know anyone willing
to take this on and get back to me.
To live next to a tree is of benefit
to the human though unless domesticated
I can't speak for the tree. In a dry landscape
there is symbiosis. My shade for your drink.
My leaf-fall for your blanket.

Jane told me rocks speak, but utter only one
word every fifty years. There are limits,
units of time outside human patience.
For the psyche ten years is nothing.
A cottonwood grows considerably in ten years.
They grow fast, live well and wildly, by the Rio Grande,
say, or next to our yard. Die young in tree years.
Often a branch breaks due to rot. Within
that break nests for bees, home for birds.

Willie Picaro knows of a tree filled with bees.
Another tree he has walked right up
its bowed limb to fetch a ball caught
in its branches. The tree, unlike Willie
Picaro, has no mother or cousin, checkbook
or fiancée. Each tree seems a greatness,
isolate, ungendered. It tenders us. Breaks us, breaks
gusts of wind. Shades and sings, it snaps, it whistles.
It never chimes or tells clocks time, but slower
time by season. We feel for it but have no way

of knowing what trees feel. Wasn't there spurious
Russian research about singing to plants?
I talk to my yeast so the bread will rise.
Both my garden and children grow
with benevolent neglect and worry,
a strange diet. They have their own agenda.
We cannot interview a tree, only admire, be
in great gratitude, not ask a thing.
They deliver without supplication.

Something Beautiful

Violence can be very grotesque and also intensely attractive. What interests me is how the two—beauty and violence—live side by side, and how moments can be created and erased almost simultaneously.
—Ori Gersht in *Smithsonian Magazine*

Imagine something beautiful,
either a cornflower or black walnut,
a tea rose, a ceramic vase glazed white.
Imagine a pea flower, a baby asleep, embroidered
shoes. Go on a holiday in Greece. Hang
a hammock between two Yucatan trees.

Now, next to it place something terrible.
What you don't want to know, what you can't
handle. The bomb for starts. Its awe and bane.
Click into black widow, drive-by shootings,
AIDS. Hundreds of rattlesnakes squirm through
years of light. Child molestation, I can't go on
to burns from cigarettes,

now shuffle. Calendula leprosy cougar
toxic waste columbines strychnine the sea.
Great Barrier Reef swarming with fish
blindness from syphilis. Imagine salmon
tarantula moon, this pattern, light dark,
dark light, dark dark. The shadows
in woods under aspen, it's dapple.

You can rely on evil. Pernicious arrivals
of goat's head seeds as sure as illuminated
manuscripts by Blake. Moments of personal grace.
Angels and gargoyles will point out the sights.
Now they cross over, code switch, you don't know
what to hold in mind, the ocean with its plastic reefs,
paintings by Georgia O'Keeffe, smoking kief,
this habitat we make of our habitual beliefs,
the porcelain vase crazed or carved
in bas relief.

Answer Me This*

Peace isn't a placebo.
Haven't we swallowed the threat of war?
And don't men want to make peace with women
and aren't women full of peace
as they fill with babies
and aren't babies made of molecules of peace
and aren't babies fools who babble on in peace
through guns and bombs? And wouldn't you try
and wage peace and didn't your grandmother?
And wasn't she Hungarian, and knew too much of war?

Isn't adobe made of mud and straw
and isn't my heart? And isn't a fire made of wood
and light and don't walks eventually turn
into flight and isn't it grand the way peace trickles
from my hands? And isn't recycling a word
for pop cans and yesterday's news and not
for the element Plutonium. And isn't Plutonium
named after Pluto, god of the Underworld:
that place you turn when there is no way up?

And couldn't Los Alamos finally turn
the way cottonwoods do in fall
to the using of sun for heat and ways
to make fuel out of music? And do you want
your children downwind of peace or downwind
of preparations for war? And isn't peace a reason
for churches and don't you want to be downwind
of God and aren't you already?

* This poem was written in 1990 for a public hearing on the proposed Special
Nuclear Materials facility at Los Alamos National Laboratories. While unhappily the
names of the countries can change, the plea is still applicable.

I want to go on record saying *Place me
downwind of peace.* How does it feel
downwind? No difference in the scent
of lilacs, no change in the wind after rain.
Don't you really want to plant gardens
and isn't the economy less fragile
than the earth and why is it money always?

I implore the crystalline minds of science
to turn to the joy of salvation,
a New World Series, Super Bowl of Peace.
And aren't tears carriers of peace
and isn't disease like war and don't you think?
And why haven't you become vegetarian again
and haven't your friends told you, "Chill!"
And hasn't war gone out of fashion like
mid-calf hemlines? Aren't Afghanistan,
Darfur, and Iraq due for something
that sings like birds and isn't that something
that sings the bird call of peace?

Humanity's Ethical Will

I will you. I will love you.
I will love you and leave you.
I will that your will be mingled
with my will. I will destroy you,
I will eat you for snack.
I will bless you. I will desecrate
your graves. I will drape your tombs
with red and gold silk that held
rose blossoms for a hundred days.
I will break bread with you.
I will break in your skull.
I will kiss you before and after
all manner of acts. I will sting.
I will be a bee in your bonnet,
a nest of wasps, alas and alack,
I will yen for you. I will raise you
from the dead. I will annihilate you.
I will be kind in my annihilation.
I will be cruel in my resurrection.
I will be simple to your complexity,
confuse your clarity. I will age.
I will grow youthful beside you.
I will divest myself of stocks
and bonds. I will donate money
to your charities. I will foul
your sacred lake. I will baptize
your child that came so late.
I will make maps of your trails
and burn them as you walk. I will
pollute the Pacific. I will pollute
the Atlantic. I will wipe the oil spill
from the sea lion's back. I will
atomic bomb you. I will practice
bombs like piano scales. I will invest
my money in plutonium. I will say matins

and vespers, pray before meals.
I will copulate with no godliness.
I will enter you like Paradise.
I will be washed up. I will complete
no task. I will *I and Thou* you.
I will *I and It* you. These
are our acts on this earth.

Thou and Thou

In this firm and wholesome chronicle the You-moments appear as queer lyric-dramatic episodes. Their spell may be seductive, but they pull us dangerously to extremes, loosening the well-tried structure, leaving behind more doubt than satisfaction, shaking up our security—altogether uncanny, altogether indispensable.
—Martin Buber, *I and Thou*

If we were friends in old Berlin
on opposite sides of the wall
or in Czechoslovakia after the velvet fell.
If we shared a hospital room

on opposite sides of the wall,
or if you were a man instead,
if we shared a hotel room,
if due to circumstance we never met.

If you were a woman instead,
a sidelong glance in the night.
If due to circumstance we never met.
If I paid money to you and you put out

a sidelong glance in the night,
the most insignificant jot of gesture.
If I paid money to you and you refused
and it stayed in flirt and portent

the most insignificant jot of gesture
is to slit light when we're alive.
To stay in flirt and portent
is the grave, just ask William Blake.

Slit light while we're alone,
slide an envelope under the door
into the grave. Just ask William Blake
what laughter vaulted from his final mouth.

Slide an envelope under my door.
Write love letters under my dress,
what laughter vaults out of our mouths
makes a medicine bundle of words.

Write love letters under my dress
or in Czechoslovakia after the velvet fell.
Drink a medicine bottle of worlds
as if we were friends in old Berlin.

That Other Woman

She leans into the Old Testament.
She puts her weight against Moses,
lifts angels with her breath. Her
ancestors applaud from Poland.

She supports the Dharma
with her laundry. Her children
gather rainbows from Taos
and string their guitars.

She lets her head fall on Jacob's shoulder.
Her habitat is wild iris above Santa Barbara
campground. Purple under investigation.
Deep as clothing wet after first rain.

The season between lightning and no
lightning supports her habit of praising.
Her hair is the Bosque, habitat for grouse.
Imagine the mint condition of her attention.

Like lilacs she praises by scent.
Like oceans she praises by sound.
Like coffee, by taste, and eye to eye,
the one receiving and the other submitting

to her magnetic will, she praises
in vision. You find your loveliest hour.
Your heart like a prayer wheel. Your face
like a drum. Tender beliefs, white prayer flags.

You mind a Himalaya that foot by foot
she helps you scale. That other woman
leans against you, grace note by grace note.
Sings you into being.

Shadow Work

For the Judith at Cortez Island

She said, "You were jumping like a child.
You were giving your power to the dead gladioli.
You were crossed circuits with the soldier's boots.
I wanted a queen of the melon of you. I wanted
el Arbol and the tree of ladders." She said,
"You were a daughter of geranium weight and
quilted depth, but I wanted the thread to crochet
me eternity. I wanted an abacus of your ribs
to conduct symphonies, sound to become a mandolin
the fish could swim." She said, "I like your poems
but your presence was crackling cellophane, a paper safe
when I wanted the sitar. I wanted the broken
column that stood beneath Frida Kahlo's head.

I wanted the spider to weave your face a moon
strand by strand, your bright reflective gaze.
No!" she said, "I wanted you to be the moon's last
laugh. To stop reflecting purses, frogs, and pain.
To generate compliments and silhouettes.
To carve sonatas in the bark of locust and invite
kingfishers to fly out of your brain." She said,
"I want more from you than you can give.
I want diamond sutras of friendship, medicine
bottles filled with flowers all in deep bloom.

I am removing the dimmer switch. I am escalating
the stakes." She said, "Become the Queen of England.
Become the lioness of violins. Become, once more,
the ringing palace bells. You're all cross-purposes
and head-lit deer, a bastardized version of a holy text."
She said, and I have to admit I sought her advice,
"I see you other than you are. I see you hold yourself
back with a plastic waist. I see you ostracized
by a leaden foot and a skitterish mind." For I had
asked and then I gave her thanks.

She was the one I chose for this particular taste.
I said, "Give me the shadow that I see
in your beautiful face."

The Arsenic Lobster of Lorca

When the lobster falls on your head (it will be a moment
of Great Awakening. A man walking out the door
into an avocado. A woman who cried tears of vinegar
into the oil of love. Maybe the telegram arrives
and your son is no longer a soldier. A war is declared
and the birds bear arms.

Or, he simply says, "I'm bored," and with those
tame words an apocalypse. Or she gets a biopsy
and it's benign. Or not. The room clears
at the mention of the word *floozy*. Any of this
and then maybe the lobster himself. Too large
for the restaurant tanks in Granada. So large
they let him go. Perhaps he was Lorca's lobster
who escaped the Civil War. Who emerged un-shot
from Fuente Grande, Fountain of Tears.
Who can stand in olive groves of Alfacar,
and for one cycle of the moon hold
the tail of crustaceans in her hands?

Maybe the arsenic was eaten and remains
in our body biding its sanguine time.
It could be the first intercourse of an angel.
It could be the longing for absurdity, Salvador Dalí
capitulated and it was a different story.
I come in after the rain of moustaches.
I shake off my fur in the valley of the shadow
of abundant figs. I hypnotize the glaciers
to stay put at the Poles. I pray. Maybe I pray.

Maybe the lobster is a deformed prayer answered
not a prayer ignored. Maybe the lobster
was poisoned by the lies of the political.
Maybe by the geothermal pools of Ojo Caliente
where arsenic is the hottest. All I know
is this: one day a giant arsenic lobster
is predicted to fall from the Andalusian sky.)
Be vigilant. Be ready for the catch.

Translating Neruda with No Spanish of My Own

The glass is white and the color of smoke is inconsequential.
Windows don't lie, have no eyelashes so they are asleep
required to stare and do a day job.

At night glass is a mirror or a spy. I like spying
so it is good I live in the country. I have changed
my chair to make a mirror of the night.

Of the day a scenery of branch and bird.
I thank Neruda every chance I get and can't get
close enough to his voice. I never heard him living

only heard him once as an echo and a shadow.
I kiss Neruda in his sleep knowing I won't wake him,
kissing the glass I leave lip prints I rub off with my thumb.

My throat is not numb. It has Neruda's imprint, green
and wild as the shore of Chile, long thin throat.
This is a translation of glass and air.

What Is

So this is the way fear ends.
So this is the way a ribbon wraps a bomb.
So this is the way a terrorist says good-bye
to his mother, the way his mother reacts to the news.
So this is an Israeli. So this is an angel in triage.
This is a man at his prayer, prostrate, sincere,
his facing east. So this is where I am in deep water.
So this is where the news commentator interrupts
the sitcom. So these are the M&M's I ate, red,
white, and blue, during the catastrophe. So this is Iraq.
So this is Pakistan. So this is the world Gary Snyder
predicted, instant exposure to each other's beauties
and pains. So this is my body. So this is an ankle
held up against the angle of Twin Towers. Silhouette
of wrist against New Orleans. Now we can't feel
our own pain. So this is the veil over our hearts,
like a calf born with a membrane, a baby with a caul.
Our heart must be licked. So this is the desert
I've resisted. The Hebrew language I never learned.
So this is Arabic. Ishmael and Isaac at their father's grave,
the last opportunity. So this is a man with a white beard
singing, his belly large as Ganesh. So this is the intersection
of sacred and profane, that rotund prayer, that enormous
voice, that girth of faith. That immense thank-you
I felt, that Shofar blast, that opened heart, that last
breath and that first breath. This is the name. Of Breath.

Tendril

Now you are tangled up in others and everything you do
has some weird failure in it.
—Rumi

I am tangled in family, the wild geese
Or were they sandhill cranes flying in formation,
Their wings rhythmic resonance, while everyone
I love flaps in different, difficult ways.

Sometimes I fly on one codependent wing,
Frida Kahlo the day his affair is discovered.
On the other I flap independently. I am that
Woman alone, Georgia to the tenth power.

Some days I need unceasingly.
I love this tangled-up love life of family.
The drama, the small violins. I hate the tangle
Of family, my forehead creased like a dollar bill.

I used to cry a lot. Tangled threads of tears
Stitched me from one man to the next. Now I do
All my man work with one difficult model. Darling,
I want to say but only if it's ironic not corny.

This leads me to tendrils. They live for tangle
The biologic curl, runner and desire. Morning
Glory and honeysuckle. Sometimes I untangle
Them and redirect to trellis or string. All I can do.

Now you have experienced the exigencies of family
And each moment may be doomed. I don't know
What *exigency* means or how to spell it.
We have to reach for what our mind can wrap around.

Chinese New Year

What wisdom can you find that is greater than kindness?
—Jean-Jacques Rousseau

I'm not sure there's a night of civility
left in me. Red tassels and crepe paper hang

in my friends' old house. I admonish myself to be polite.
Enamel over my natural tendencies.

The greeting for the New Year offers increase.
Broken cookies predict twice, "You will make

new friends." My old friend rubs my back,
if not now when? We laugh. Why do Jews

love Chinese food above their own? I love
propriety, but more than that the chance to spill

a bit into new ears. The eyes of depth. *The ribbon
of gold from the sun is a thousand miles long,*

says the scroll of the Yangtze. Not my river,
but the Allegheny is, spoken of over tea.

The sea bass came apart at the touch.
The ginger stung my tongue. If only sweets

were all, but we've come to expect a serving
of Open Sesame. At home I am alone.

There is nobody greeting me, needing a shred
of red meat. I turn on the TV. I read at books.

The gathering did me good. Underneath
sleep is dreams. Underneath darkness is gold.

My heart, red as a lantern,
hangs in an old room.

Gezundheit

Leaving home is the sneeze that jolts me
out of the predictable. *God Bless You,*
people say as I walk out, cast into the world
by my abrupt thrust. October.

The cottonwoods caw, *yellow, yellow,* with a beauty
so severe it's almost obscene, the S and M
of transience. I move north, walk through
people I've met before. *Hello Hello.*

A woman missing most of her teeth is stitching
yucca onto canvas. All of this is the *God
Bless You* of breathing out. At home,
the inhalation. I come and go, arrive,

depart. Inhabit my body like a house,
my bed like a shroud, practice small good-byes.
The extroverted moments of sun, the introverted
motion of eyes over pages. I drive in and out

a thousand places of eyes. A million mistakes.
But this week in the vast outer I found the hidden,
the Hebrew song that moved my cells into beautiful
regalia of DNA, aligned my spine, certified

my chakras, made me Jew for that day, scented
me holy. I stood. I sat. I touched the Torah
with a prayer shawl I had sewn by my own hand
a dozen years before. I felt remembered as I let

my mother and my father come to me in their new
forms. It's the coming and going. Introvert. Extrovert.
Which breath is your mother? Where are your father's
celestial neckties? The ten Days of Awe spread out

on the table, a calendar of blessings. How did I forget
my name? What date did God miss? How many right
hands make war? How much peace is possible, even
here, even now? Even over there in the mangers of war?

Concert

The drummer from Egypt leaves his *doumbek*
Resting on its head. He finds it full of chicken bones.
Fill it with money. No, fill it with love.
How little we know of the innards of others.

I am flashing photos of my grandson.
The gesture says, do not ever make him a soldier.
My daughter's friend is afraid of terrorists.
My daughter says, I'm afraid of patriotism.

I find the passport my grandmother used
To return to Romania in the thirties
With Ida, her youngest. Ida calls today.
Her son arranges music for the army band.

It was that or Vietnam. Her throat thickens.
My mother's voice with age and all the residual love.
Cleanse your palate between one world and the next.
Make love, give birth, die a little.

A man I never saw smile is grinning.
He must be listening to something else
Than the news, the stock market report,
All the obituaries for God.

Leila means "one night." What do we have besides one?
My teacher taught the seven holy vowels, never
Forget "ahhh." Singing of the earth,
Welcome of the baby to the new mother.

This music from the beleaguered Middle East
Not one mention of peace, but we make a feast
Of peace. They take four encores, Egypt,
Morocco, and two impossible scores.

Let's go on vacation with those we love most.
The yellow leaves of river trees. A tumbleweed
Is also the burning bush. Look outside.
The Tree of Life is blazing.

Joining Rabia on Eid

For Rabia Van Hattum

Next to Karima in the yurt, I like sitting with the women.
A little girl in a white lacy dress twirls,
Offering seeds, placing her white stockinged feet in my lap.
Islam is two women passing baked goods

And a little girl in a white lacy dress twirling.
My legs crossed under me, I've sat among women before.
Islam is two women playing hand drums.
Sugared ginger, dry mango, this heart is sweet and burnt.

My legs, stumbling, have walked the White City before.
Have you seen the black rocks lodged in the fissures?
Sugared ginger, dry mango, this land is sweet and burnt.
I never meant to lose God in the crack of the familiar.

Have you seen the black rock lodged in the fissures?
The man in white will slaughter a sheep tomorrow.
I never meant to lose God in the cracks of family.
If failure is enough, surely success is more.

That man in the white scarf will sacrifice a sheep.
Please come back and eat with us, I can smell it roasting.
If failure is a meal, success is a feast.
A child with a somber face reminds me wars are all lost.

Please come eat with us, you'd be most welcome.
I once heard three drummers inside these tent walls.
A child with a somber face belies the need for wars.
"How can we call ourselves civilized?" Naomi asks.

I heard drummers from Egypt inside these tent walls.
When we take off our shoes we can't run away.
"How can we call ourselves civilized?" the poet asks.
I'm offered a part of myself I forgot.

When we take off our shoes we can't run away,
Offering seeds, placing her white stockinged feet in my hands
I'm offered a part of myself I forgot.
Next to Karima, sitting with the women in the yurt.

The Strange Guest

The Persian bride slept at my house
on her wedding night, alone,

though we were strangers the day before.
This marriage of hers was off dancing

in the world while she slept on my sofa
to the sounds of the dishwasher rinsing dreams.

She placed her hand on my heart, between
my breasts and said, "There is a sad eye here

though the architecture of the mind is wondrous."
She asked me to laugh, after all,

it is her wedding night, the most
beautiful wedding she has ever seen.

My trust and distrust dance
like an aunt from the bride's side

and an uncle from the groom's,
and I do laugh because she's a bride.

My family sits nearby and my old groom says
how beautiful I look in her hands.

Never stop opening
your house to strangers

and feeding them the last fruits
of the garden, nasturtium flowers and tea

made with honey from your oldest neighbor's bees.
Don't stop moving your hand to your heart.

Say "Yes!" when the bride wants to impose.
You never know what the stranger has to give

or better still what rice you have to throw.

Wedding Poem

For Mirabai and Eddie Daniels, 1998

After so many years, what if
we decide once and for all to wed?

We were searching for the true,
the Absolute. All the time it was our self

we were searching for, our sweetness
and ability to change.

We go on marrying and divorcing
each other, and ourselves, constantly

just as we die and are reborn 7,000 times
in each breath. In marriage there is a breathing

that occurs at night, when there is no
He or She, dark that takes and gives

despite our best and worst intentions.
Even our moods and methods make no claims.

Our intelligent heart requires a slumber.
So go on waking, go on sleeping

together and whole communities are made
out of the awakening. Whole landscapes

delight. What is. Being wed is as perfect
as being a fish or being trees on a hillside.

This is research in how, an experiment
in why and why not

and every moment is in loving or falling
apart, pleading "The One, the One."

Chicago Marriage

For Arlene and Daniel

You have been married
since before you met. Grade school
lovers preparing you for this, gathering
of grain, harvesting a city from a lake.

You will be married after you are gone.
These vows outlive the holy ones
who make them. All time resides in you
once you make a house for time.

Even when you fail, you are failing
more brilliantly. Failure is more worthy
than before with its patient earth and
laughter, reparation carried in your chest.

When you rise up living and lie down
thanking, you marry us. Community
of trees, city marries shore, animal
to salt, longing to glass of wine.

The wild flowers say, "I do."
How much can you bear? For you
have been married since before the answer,
"Yes." A ceremony before your parents

gave you breath. Your heart
is the Old Temple, how much can it hear?
City you love beside, fragrance of prayer.
Marriage contains heart of stranger,

heart of river, heart of health and illness,
heart of money, heart beating darkness,
heart beating light. Your true north and
center of the compass, place
where you have always been wed.

The Vessel

For Dana and Jessica

You think you have chosen.
You are being poured by God into a vessel.

Wedding vases from the pueblos have two spouts
but one body. You can't escape from sky and air.

Once I beaded blue and white barrettes for your blond hair,
when the grass came up to your knees.

Now you take vows. You enter a convent,
marry God, who resides in the groom.
You think you have chosen. All marriages are arranged.

My rabbi said, "Be thankful for the hard parts, not only
the good." We learn at the edge of our ability to bear.

Women from the pueblos carried water on their heads.
Some days you will move through life this carefully.

I love how impossible two people are
under one roof, drinking from one glass, balancing
checkbooks and exasperation, elongating moments

by looking them in the eye. In your sacred order
you will be polished and refined by the teachings

of this sacred other. It's the alembic where
alchemy occurs, distilling and working a change.

Your heart grows large enough to contain it all,
sickness-health, richer-poorer, a prayer, a well,
all of Chimayó, and Santuario with its endless healing dirt.

Don't believe anything I say. Open
to each other. Invent love every day.

To My Son and His Novia

This is the wild wide intimate.
You join hands, a ring from Tiffany's,
hold hands so you can dance,
then dive into mystery.

Every marriage must rhyme
because it makes no sense without
a rhythm of days and a meter of nights,
without huge love and occasional fights.

I wish you patience like the Rio Grande,
flood, and drought, everything occurs within time's
massive hand. I send blessing and a prayer,
one to bestow, the other to ask for God's infinite care.

Live in the literal and in metaphor.
If you think this is easy, you are wrong.
Yet I who am pessimistic am today an optimist.
I believe you have both found the best in each

and will grow towards that beauty, kiss
by kiss. Love each other best,
with some leftover for the world.
Don't be led astray. Recycle love. Be true

to who you are and to each quality you love
in other. Grow wise and seasoned as you hold.
This is the wild wide intimate.
You join hands, wear rings for infinity,

Conjure up bands so we can dance
and then dive into mystery.

On the Road in Green

All of the sudden hearts are green and green
hearted we Dylan Thomas onto the shoulder of the road
where we pull over and put our ear down to the soul
listen to Anne Sexton and Sylvia, a gas lassitude,
and pull ourselves up by our spiritual bootstraps and away
from the drunks, the suicides, thinking my heart is the green
model, circa Anytime, and motor off in Neal Cassady's last
convertible, skipping Mexico and going straight
to California, skipping Big Sur and going straight
to the city where we purchase on Grant Avenue
a yellow Long Life Bowl for ninety-nine cents,
and we don't buy a red one, too much like blood,
we don't buy satin slippers, we don't buy lo mein,
we don't buy rice paper wrapped in brocade or fat
brushes and black ink in a tablet embossed with a panda,
we buy white porcelain horses from when our hearts were
green as Ferlinghetti's money when he opened City Lights,
green as the stoplight at Presidio and Sutter saying, *Go Girl*
except we are women with green hearts soon
to be sixty, seventy, eighty then Love as in tennis,
meanwhile the heart goes on reciting *Leaves of Grass*
in an adolescent accent while Walt Whitman's
heart remains unsullied, I never heard a bad
word uttered against him. I forget that in Lorca
"Green, how I want you green," the green has the sense
of dying. I must see with green eyes how the money holds out
and how long the green heart sings. Sticking my thumb out
into the briny wind, get picked up by a new model, circa Now,
an invention like the perpetual motion machine of green.

Mucho Gusto

Mucho cars driving north re-create the sky's canopy.
Mucho gusto, the man says, not taking his breath, not
taking off his black death's baseball cap. Mucho
telephone lines and electric along the delicate Rios.
Mucho the crow says retreating, causing the last fall
cottonwood leaves to call down and mucho grief
the gills of the fishes in Abiquiu Lake take in pure tears.

Mucho the widow says, this is not daylight. She cannot
walk but is dancing. Mucho her father says, flying
from back east, holding her arm which weighs now mucho.
Mucho Homework, my daughter says laughing on the phone,
laughing and laughing until laughter itself loses something
in translation of childhood to adult.

Mucho dinero the bank knows we owe it, the bank
with its safety deposits of fresh figs and ancestral shadows.
Slowly we gnaw at the illusion called debt.
We deposit gratitude, that we are living and darlings.
So many departed. Some by boat and some by AIDS,
some by skateboard and some by full moon promising
greener pastures and some by overdose and some by doom
and some by politics and some who arrive and look
into the mouth of El Mundo and panic and some by camel
and some by memory and some by boat waving hasta.

Thanking each other and the hours, the mesmerized space
between us. Thanking the flavors and mucho the Cathedral
right off the Plaza and mucho the bookstores filled with
best sellers and plenty right now and plenty next lifetime.
One I love now in the plenty of afterlife. Mucho the bardos
and mucho we love and are praying. Mucho the sun of late
afternoon the week of el Dias de los Muertos and they
are playing music, and they are singing plenty.

Melted Radio, Jazz Flashlight

This morning, this Sunday, in slow drizzle
I am falling in and out of dream. With a musical score
of rain pocking the red metal roof, I can have
my father again on a road trip we never took.
I can buy gaudy jewelry at a hotel gift shop,
can dine with strangers I don't like the look of,
can repair the greenhouse, can bring the young
construction worker anything he wants
and he can promise me my turn. I tell him it isn't easy
to please me, I'm a girl. In dream I say girl.
In a dream I can pay off any debt to my waking life,
behave wildly and make terrible messes, forget
plane schedules, put my hand in anyone's pants.

While in daily life I labor to keep things together
in dreams I get to fall apart, wake again in relief.
In this way, trim and frum by day while dreams
are *sturm und drang*, free ride courtesy my unconscious.
I indulge. Nobody gets hurt. Carl Jung, I had
a close brush with the archetypes last night. I am still
wearing my blue pajamas. My parents are both
still dead and my son did not move to Farmington.
He's here down the road. It is not ten minutes to two.
I did not miss my class or fall into a hole landing on my feet.
I don't have to visit an alien emergency room.

I think I will make pancakes strewn with raspberries.
I think I will say something coy to my husband.
Today, the week of my birthday, I am utterly grateful
for these small bardos, practice runs for death,
the art of the uncontrolled, the surrealist's pet mirror,
Dada, night song, excursion ticket, Caribbean cruise,
smoked hours, medicinal vaudeville,
gas station, night horse, jazz flashlight, rapscallion.
I get to lie down thanking and rise up again.
All my days I play out demise and resurrection,
a rebirth from oblivion deeper than forgetting,
a free moon to swallow, a candle that blows ordinary out.

Mirabai's Birthday: On hearing Ram Dass had a stroke

We don't know how long
but we know we long.

The shadows of afternoon stretch
from light toward dark.

Who will comfort the dying
when the one who comforts
the dying dies?

Don't forget there's a full moon
and somewhere in the snow
it's someone's birthday.

We blow out candles
with a breath grown strong
in loving.

About the Author

JOAN LOGGHE IS POET LAUREATE for Santa Fe, 2010–2012. She works at poetry in community from La Puebla, New Mexico, where she and her husband, Michael, raised three children, built three houses, and have three grandchildren. Awards include a National Endowment for the Arts fellowship, Witter Bynner Foundation for Poetry grants, a Mabel Dodge Luhan internship, and a Barbara Deming/Money for Women grant. Selected books are *Twenty Years in Bed with the Same Man* (La Alameda, a finalist for Western States Book Award), *Blessed Resistance* (Mariposa Printing and Publishing), *Sofía* (La Alameda), and *Rice* (Tres Chicas Books). Her enthusiasm has inspired poetry in students from Santa Clara Pueblo Day School to Zagreb, Croatia, and Bratislava, Slovakia, UNM–Los Alamos and Santa Fe Community College to Santa Fe Girls' School where she has been Poet-in-Residence for ten years. With Miriam Sagan and Renée Gregorio she founded Tres Chicas Books. www.joanlogghe.com